LEE CANTER'S

RECORD BOOK
PLUS

The "3-in-1" Class Record Book

- **Academic Documentation**
- **Behavior Documentation**
- **Parent Communication Resources**

SCHOOL YEAR _____ TO _____

TEACHER _____

GRADE(S) _____

A PUBLICATION OF CANTER & ASSOCIATES

6-Year Calendar

2005

JANUARY
M T W T F S S
```
            1  2
 3  4  5  6  7  8  9
10 11 12 13 14 15 16
17 18 19 20 21 22 23
24 25 26 27 28 29 30
31
```

FEBRUARY
M T W T F S S
```
    1  2  3  4  5  6
 7  8  9 10 11 12 13
14 15 16 17 18 19 20
21 22 23 24 25 26 27
28
```

MARCH
M T W T F S S
```
    1  2  3  4  5  6
 7  8  9 10 11 12 13
14 15 16 17 18 19 20
21 22 23 24 25 26 27
28 29 30 31
```

APRIL
M T W T F S S
```
             1  2  3
 4  5  6  7  8  9 10
11 12 13 14 15 16 17
18 19 20 21 22 23 24
25 26 27 28 29 30
```

MAY
M T W T F S S
```
                   1
 2  3  4  5  6  7  8
 9 10 11 12 13 14 15
16 17 18 19 20 21 22
23 24 25 26 27 28 29
30 31
```

JUNE
M T W T F S S
```
       1  2  3  4  5
 6  7  8  9 10 11 12
13 14 15 16 17 18 19
20 21 22 23 24 25 26
27 28 29 30
```

JULY
M T W T F S S
```
             1  2  3
 4  5  6  7  8  9 10
11 12 13 14 15 16 17
18 19 20 21 22 23 24
25 26 27 28 29 30 31
```

AUGUST
M T W T F S S
```
 1  2  3  4  5  6  7
 8  9 10 11 12 13 14
15 16 17 18 19 20 21
22 23 24 25 26 27 28
29 30 31
```

SEPTEMBER
M T W T F S S
```
          1  2  3  4
 5  6  7  8  9 10 11
12 13 14 15 16 17 18
19 20 21 22 23 24 25
26 27 28 29 30
```

OCTOBER
M T W T F S S
```
                1  2
 3  4  5  6  7  8  9
10 11 12 13 14 15 16
17 18 19 20 21 22 23
24 25 26 27 28 29 30
31
```

NOVEMBER
M T W T F S S
```
    1  2  3  4  5  6
 7  8  9 10 11 12 13
14 15 16 17 18 19 20
21 22 23 24 25 26 27
28 29 30
```

DECEMBER
M T W T F S S
```
          1  2  3  4
 5  6  7  8  9 10 11
12 13 14 15 16 17 18
19 20 21 22 23 24 25
26 27 28 29 30 31
```

2006

JANUARY
M T W T F S S
```
                   1
 2  3  4  5  6  7  8
 9 10 11 12 13 14 15
16 17 18 19 20 21 22
23 24 25 26 27 28 29
30 31
```

FEBRUARY
M T W T F S S
```
       1  2  3  4  5
 6  7  8  9 10 11 12
13 14 15 16 17 18 19
20 21 22 23 24 25 26
27 28
```

MARCH
M T W T F S S
```
       1  2  3  4  5
 6  7  8  9 10 11 12
13 14 15 16 17 18 19
20 21 22 23 24 25 26
27 28 29 30 31
```

APRIL
M T W T F S S
```
                1  2
 3  4  5  6  7  8  9
10 11 12 13 14 15 16
17 18 19 20 21 22 23
24 25 26 27 28 29 30
```

MAY
M T W T F S S
```
 1  2  3  4  5  6  7
 8  9 10 11 12 13 14
15 16 17 18 19 20 21
22 23 24 25 26 27 28
29 30 31
```

JUNE
M T W T F S S
```
          1  2  3  4
 5  6  7  8  9 10 11
12 13 14 15 16 17 18
19 20 21 22 23 24 25
26 27 28 29 30
```

JULY
M T W T F S S
```
                1  2
 3  4  5  6  7  8  9
10 11 12 13 14 15 16
17 18 19 20 21 22 23
24 25 26 27 28 29 30
31
```

AUGUST
M T W T F S S
```
    1  2  3  4  5  6
 7  8  9 10 11 12 13
14 15 16 17 18 19 20
21 22 23 24 25 26 27
28 29 30 31
```

SEPTEMBER
M T W T F S S
```
             1  2  3
 4  5  6  7  8  9 10
11 12 13 14 15 16 17
18 19 20 21 22 23 24
25 26 27 28 29 30
```

OCTOBER
M T W T F S S
```
                   1
 2  3  4  5  6  7  8
 9 10 11 12 13 14 15
16 17 18 19 20 21 22
23 24 25 26 27 28 29
30 31
```

NOVEMBER
M T W T F S S
```
       1  2  3  4  5
 6  7  8  9 10 11 12
13 14 15 16 17 18 19
20 21 22 23 24 25 26
27 28 29 30
```

DECEMBER
M T W T F S S
```
             1  2  3
 4  5  6  7  8  9 10
11 12 13 14 15 16 17
18 19 20 21 22 23 24
25 26 27 28 29 30 31
```

2007

JANUARY
M T W T F S S
```
 1  2  3  4  5  6  7
 8  9 10 11 12 13 14
15 16 17 18 19 20 21
22 23 24 25 26 27 28
29 30 31
```

FEBRUARY
M T W T F S S
```
          1  2  3  4
 5  6  7  8  9 10 11
12 13 14 15 16 17 18
19 20 21 22 23 24 25
26 27 28
```

MARCH
M T W T F S S
```
          1  2  3  4
 5  6  7  8  9 10 11
12 13 14 15 16 17 18
19 20 21 22 23 24 25
26 27 28 29 30 31
```

APRIL
M T W T F S S
```
                   1
 2  3  4  5  6  7  8
 9 10 11 12 13 14 15
16 17 18 19 20 21 22
23 24 25 26 27 28 29
30
```

MAY
M T W T F S S
```
    1  2  3  4  5  6
 7  8  9 10 11 12 13
14 15 16 17 18 19 20
21 22 23 24 25 26 27
28 29 30 31
```

JUNE
M T W T F S S
```
             1  2  3
 4  5  6  7  8  9 10
11 12 13 14 15 16 17
18 19 20 21 22 23 24
25 26 27 28 29 30
```

JULY
M T W T F S S
```
                1  2
 3  4  5  6  7  8  9
10 11 12 13 14 15 16
17 18 19 20 21 22 23
24 25 26 27 28 29 30
31
```

AUGUST
M T W T F S S
```
       1  2  3  4  5
 6  7  8  9 10 11 12
13 14 15 16 17 18 19
20 21 22 23 24 25 26
27 28 29 30 31
```

SEPTEMBER
M T W T F S S
```
                1  2
 3  4  5  6  7  8  9
10 11 12 13 14 15 16
17 18 19 20 21 22 23
24 25 26 27 28 29 30
```

OCTOBER
M T W T F S S
```
 1  2  3  4  5  6  7
 8  9 10 11 12 13 14
15 16 17 18 19 20 21
22 23 24 25 26 27 28
29 30 31
```

NOVEMBER
M T W T F S S
```
          1  2  3  4
 5  6  7  8  9 10 11
12 13 14 15 16 17 18
19 20 21 22 23 24 25
26 27 28 29 30
```

DECEMBER
M T W T F S S
```
                1  2
 3  4  5  6  7  8  9
10 11 12 13 14 15 16
17 18 19 20 21 22 23
24 25 26 27 28 29 30
31
```

2008

JANUARY
M T W T F S S
```
    1  2  3  4  5  6
 7  8  9 10 11 12 13
14 15 16 17 18 19 20
21 22 23 24 25 26 27
28 29 30 31
```

FEBRUARY
M T W T F S S
```
             1  2  3
 4  5  6  7  8  9 10
11 12 13 14 15 16 17
18 19 20 21 22 23 24
25 26 27 28 29
```

MARCH
M T W T F S S
```
                1  2
 3  4  5  6  7  8  9
10 11 12 13 14 15 16
17 18 19 20 21 22 23
24 25 26 27 28 29 30
31
```

APRIL
M T W T F S S
```
    1  2  3  4  5  6
 7  8  9 10 11 12 13
14 15 16 17 18 19 20
21 22 23 24 25 26 27
28 29 30
```

MAY
M T W T F S S
```
          1  2  3  4
 5  6  7  8  9 10 11
12 13 14 15 16 17 18
19 20 21 22 23 24 25
26 27 28 29 30 31
```

JUNE
M T W T F S S
```
                   1
 2  3  4  5  6  7  8
 9 10 11 12 13 14 15
16 17 18 19 20 21 22
23 24 25 26 27 28 29
30
```

JULY
M T W T F S S
```
    1  2  3  4  5  6
 7  8  9 10 11 12 13
14 15 16 17 18 19 20
21 22 23 24 25 26 27
28 29 30 31
```

AUGUST
M T W T F S S
```
             1  2  3
 4  5  6  7  8  9 10
11 12 13 14 15 16 17
18 19 20 21 22 23 24
25 26 27 28 29 30 31
```

SEPTEMBER
M T W T F S S
```
 1  2  3  4  5  6  7
 8  9 10 11 12 13 14
15 16 17 18 19 20 21
22 23 24 25 26 27 28
29 30
```

OCTOBER
M T W T F S S
```
          1  2  3  4
 5  6  7  8  9 10 11
12 13 14 15 16 17 18
19 20 21 22 23 24 25
26 27 28 29 30 31
```

NOVEMBER
M T W T F S S
```
                1  2
 3  4  5  6  7  8  9
10 11 12 13 14 15 16
17 18 19 20 21 22 23
24 25 26 27 28 29 30
```

DECEMBER
M T W T F S S
```
 1  2  3  4  5  6  7
 8  9 10 11 12 13 14
15 16 17 18 19 20 21
22 23 24 25 26 27 28
29 30 31
```

2009

JANUARY
M T W T F S S
```
          1  2  3  4
 5  6  7  8  9 10 11
12 13 14 15 16 17 18
19 20 21 22 23 24 25
26 27 28 29 30 31
```

FEBRUARY
M T W T F S S
```
                   1
 2  3  4  5  6  7  8
 9 10 11 12 13 14 15
16 17 18 19 20 21 22
23 24 25 26 27 28
```

MARCH
M T W T F S S
```
                   1
 2  3  4  5  6  7  8
 9 10 11 12 13 14 15
16 17 18 19 20 21 22
23 24 25 26 27 28 29
30 31
```

APRIL
M T W T F S S
```
       1  2  3  4  5
 6  7  8  9 10 11 12
13 14 15 16 17 18 19
20 21 22 23 24 25 26
27 28 29 30
```

MAY
M T W T F S S
```
             1  2  3
 4  5  6  7  8  9 10
11 12 13 14 15 16 17
18 19 20 21 22 23 24
25 26 27 28 29 30 31
```

JUNE
M T W T F S S
```
 1  2  3  4  5  6  7
 8  9 10 11 12 13 14
15 16 17 18 19 20 21
22 23 24 25 26 27 28
29 30
```

JULY
M T W T F S S
```
          1  2  3  4
 5  6  7  8  9 10 11
12 13 14 15 16 17 18
19 20 21 22 23 24 25
26 27 28 29 30 31
```

AUGUST
M T W T F S S
```
             1  2
 3  4  5  6  7  8  9
10 11 12 13 14 15 16
17 18 19 20 21 22 23
24 25 26 27 28 29 30
31
```

SEPTEMBER
M T W T F S S
```
    1  2  3  4  5  6
 7  8  9 10 11 12 13
14 15 16 17 18 19 20
21 22 23 24 25 26 27
28 29 30
```

OCTOBER
M T W T F S S
```
          1  2  3  4
 5  6  7  8  9 10 11
12 13 14 15 16 17 18
19 20 21 22 23 24 25
26 27 28 29 30 31
```

NOVEMBER
M T W T F S S
```
                1  2
 3  4  5  6  7  8  9
10 11 12 13 14 15 16
17 18 19 20 21 22 23
24 25 26 27 28 29 30
```

DECEMBER
M T W T F S S
```
    1  2  3  4  5  6
 7  8  9 10 11 12 13
14 15 16 17 18 19 20
21 22 23 24 25 26 27
28 29 30 31
```

2010

JANUARY
M T W T F S S
```
             1  2  3
 4  5  6  7  8  9 10
11 12 13 14 15 16 17
18 19 20 21 22 23 24
25 26 27 28 29 30 31
```

FEBRUARY
M T W T F S S
```
 1  2  3  4  5  6  7
 8  9 10 11 12 13 14
15 16 17 18 19 20 21
22 23 24 25 26 27 28
```

MARCH
M T W T F S S
```
 1  2  3  4  5  6  7
 8  9 10 11 12 13 14
15 16 17 18 19 20 21
22 23 24 25 26 27 28
29 30 31
```

APRIL
M T W T F S S
```
          1  2  3  4
 5  6  7  8  9 10 11
12 13 14 15 16 17 18
19 20 21 22 23 24 25
26 27 28 29 30
```

MAY
M T W T F S S
```
                1  2
 3  4  5  6  7  8  9
10 11 12 13 14 15 16
17 18 19 20 21 22 23
24 25 26 27 28 29 30
31
```

JUNE
M T W T F S S
```
    1  2  3  4  5  6
 7  8  9 10 11 12 13
14 15 16 17 18 19 20
21 22 23 24 25 26 27
28 29 30
```

JULY
M T W T F S S
```
             1  2  3  4
 5  6  7  8  9 10 11
12 13 14 15 16 17 18
19 20 21 22 23 24 25
26 27 28 29 30 31
```

AUGUST
M T W T F S S
```
                   1
 2  3  4  5  6  7  8
 9 10 11 12 13 14 15
16 17 18 19 20 21 22
23 24 25 26 27 28 29
30 31
```

SEPTEMBER
M T W T F S S
```
       1  2  3  4  5
 6  7  8  9 10 11 12
13 14 15 16 17 18 19
20 21 22 23 24 25 26
27 28 29 30
```

OCTOBER
M T W T F S S
```
             1  2  3
 4  5  6  7  8  9 10
11 12 13 14 15 16 17
18 19 20 21 22 23 24
25 26 27 28 29 30 31
```

NOVEMBER
M T W T F S S
```
 1  2  3  4  5  6  7
 8  9 10 11 12 13 14
15 16 17 18 19 20 21
22 23 24 25 26 27 28
29 30
```

DECEMBER
M T W T F S S
```
       1  2  3  4  5
 6  7  8  9 10 11 12
13 14 15 16 17 18 19
20 21 22 23 24 25 26
27 28 29 30 31
```

PD4167 3/05

Table of Contents

Record Book Plus Overview 4

Section One—Academic Documentation
How Academic Documentation Sheets Will Help You 7
Suggested Uses for Traditional Grading Sheets 9
Suggested Uses for Open-Ended Grading Sheets 10
Traditional Grading Sheets
Open-Ended Grading Sheets

Section Two—Behavior Documentation
How Behavior Documentation Sheets Will Help You 103
How to Use the Behavior Documentation Sheet 105
Behavior Documentation Sheets

Section Three—Parent Communication Resources
How to Develop Effective Partnerships with Parents 147
Communicating with Parents—All Year Long! 148
Conducting Effective Parent Conferences 149
What to Say During a Parent Conference 150
Contacting Parents at the First Sign of a Problem 151
Working with Parents to Solve Persistent Problems 152
Sample Problem-Solving Conference 153
Problem-Solving Conference Planning Sheet (reproducible) 155
How to Handle Difficult Situations with Parents 156
Positive Parent Communication Logs 159
Class Roster ....Inside Back Cover

RECORD BOOK PLUS

Three special sections add up to increased parent involvement and greater student success.

1 Academic Documentation

Traditional and open-ended grading sheets for all your recordkeeping needs:

- Letter Grades
- Number Grades
- Comments
- Group Evaluations
- Portfolio Assessments

Teacher Tips to help you:

- improve academic grades.
- encourage responsible behavior.
- increase parent support.

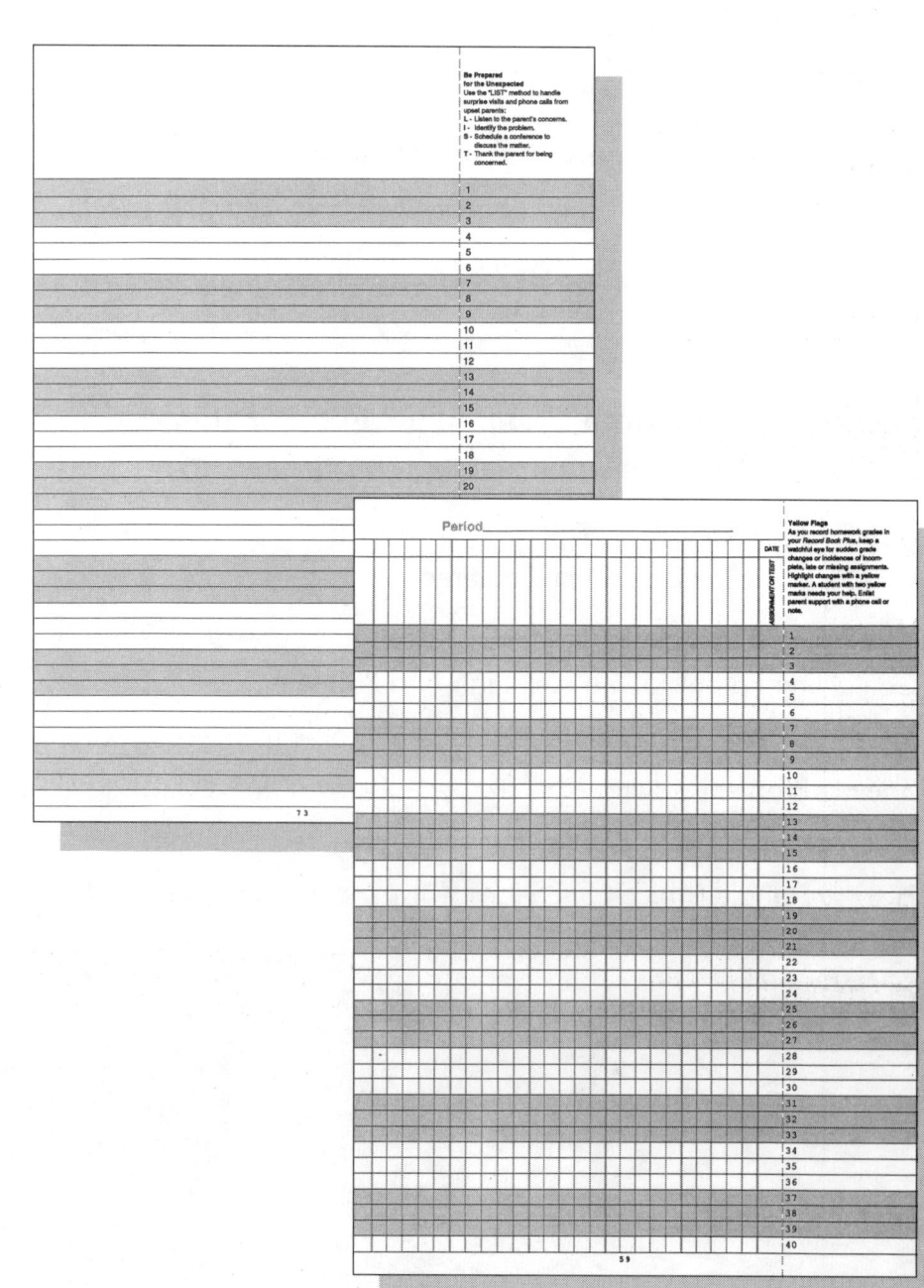

2 Behavior Documentation

Behavior Documentation Sheets provide an ongoing record of:

- a student's problem behavior.
- a student's positive behavior.
- specific actions taken with a student.
- parent contact.
- follow-up actions taken.
- parent conference notes.

Guidelines explain why, when and how to document problems and positives.

Behavior Documentation Sheet

Student_____ Parent(s)_____
Grade_____ Home Phone_____ Work Phone_____

Date of Entry	+ / ✓	Reason for Documentation Describe the positive or problem behavior. What did you observe? List facts.	Actions Taken with Student Describe in detail disciplinary actions taken or positive reinforcement given.	Parent Contact Note (N) Phone (P) Other (O)	Follow Up Record input received from parent. Describe actions you and parent will take to ensure future success.

Parent Conference Notes   Date_____   Parent Conference Notes   Date_____

146

...ntation Sheets

...now about their children's ups and downs—
...d behaviorally. They need to know when a problem
...problem is being handled, and what they can do to
...eed to hear about their children's positive behavior
...cesses can be recognized and reinforced at home.

...factual behavior documentation gives you the tools
...d professionally work with parents for the benefit of

...e Support

...volved in the behavior-management loop, your
...ds to know the nature of a student's behavior
...occurred, and what actions you have taken with
...parents) to solve the problem. Your objective
...dent's behavior (documented on the Behavior
...heet) will be invaluable in getting your administrator
...problem-solving process.

...avior entries on the Behavior Documentation Sheets
...behavior, noteworthy improvements, awards)
...l with your administrator so that additional student
...parent communication can be provided on an
...el.

...ices Support

...ctual data is essential for a student to qualify
...ces such as special education, speech and
...ce counseling, and remedial reading. By using
...umentation Sheets to keep consistent, dated
...l performance and your attempts to deal with
...ill speed up the referral process and get the help
...s need.

104

Positive Parent Communication Log

Use this sheet to keep track of your positive parent communications.
List students' names. Record date of contact. Indicate method of contact: (P) Phone or (N) Note - like this: 11/3 P

Student Names

...th Parents

**...mmunication:
...he Better!**

...ne each parent before school begins to introduce
...ssage you send is clear—"I care about your child."

...gins, or during the first week of school, send home a
...y your hopes and plans for the upcoming school year.

...ew weeks of school, send home a positive note or make
...each parent, detailing a success their child has had in
...completed all her classwork the first week of school. You
...of such responsible behavior."

...kes It Happen

...Communication Logs on pages 159 and 160 to keep
...sitive communication. Plan to make a specific number of
...calls each day. (Just two calls a day reach 40 parents in

...mple supply of positive notes and keep them handy.
...tes when students return from lunch recess to jot down
...tes. (Three notes a day reach 60 parents a month.)
...sitive communication time into your daily lesson plans.
...are scheduled, they happen!

...ers about Positive Communication

...n describing a student's positive behavior, talent or
...r. "Robert contributed many interesting facts about
...ur science discussion today."

...s into the message. Describe how you feel about the
...s behavior. "It's such a pleasure to have Robert in class.
...siasm stimulates interest and creativity in other students."

- Share the joy. Ask the parent to share the content of your conversation (or note) with the student. "Please tell Robert that I called and that I am very pleased with his participation in class."
- Thank parents for their support. Parents help in so many ways— encouraging, nudging, and supporting their child's efforts. Make sure you acknowledge their help with an appreciative word.

148

---

3 Parent Communication Resources

Ideas and guidelines for using academic and behavior documentation to:

- develop and maintain positive home-school communication all year long.
- conduct successful parent conferences.
- enlist parent support at the first sign of a problem.
- plan and conduct a productive problem-solving conference.
- handle difficult situations with parents.

ACADEMIC DOCUMENTATION

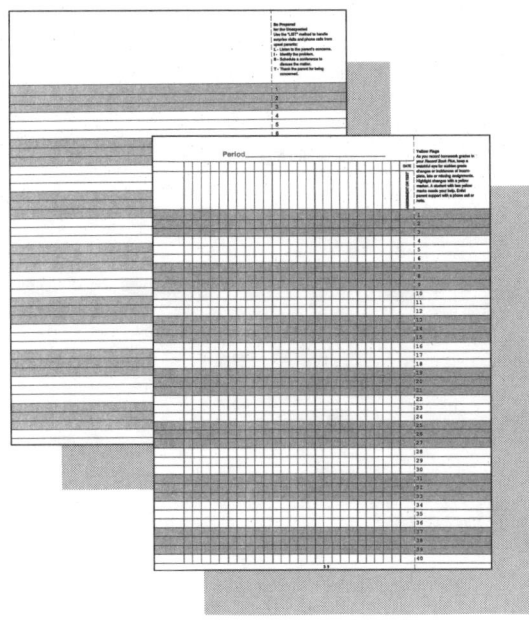

Use your academic grading sheets to:

- Monitor student progress and regularly update parents throughout the year.

- Report student academic progress to parents and enlist their support in problem areas.

- Identify a student's academic weaknesses and enlist the help of necessary school personnel (administrator, specialists, counselor).

RECORD BOOK *PLUS'*
Two Versatile Grading Sheets

- Thirty 10-week grading sheets to accommodate all traditional recordkeeping and grading needs

- Terrific teacher tips—a new tip on each grading spread

- Subject/period notations

- Perforated student lists

- Assignment/test notations

Traditional Grading Sheets

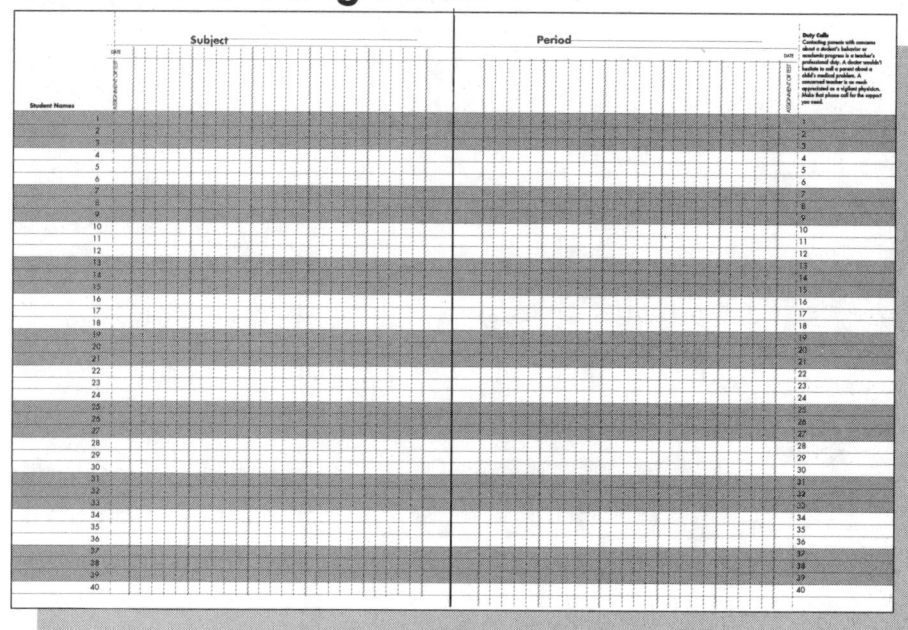

- Thirty-one grading pages with open-ended design for unlimited custom tailoring to fit your ever-changing assessment needs

- Terrific teacher tips—a new tip on each grading spread

- Perforated student lists

- Grading spaces just the size you need for:

  — Written evaluations

  — Cooperative learning-group assessments

  — Multi-purpose assignment evaluations

  — Whole language evaluations

  — Integrated curriculum notes

Open-Ended Grading Sheets

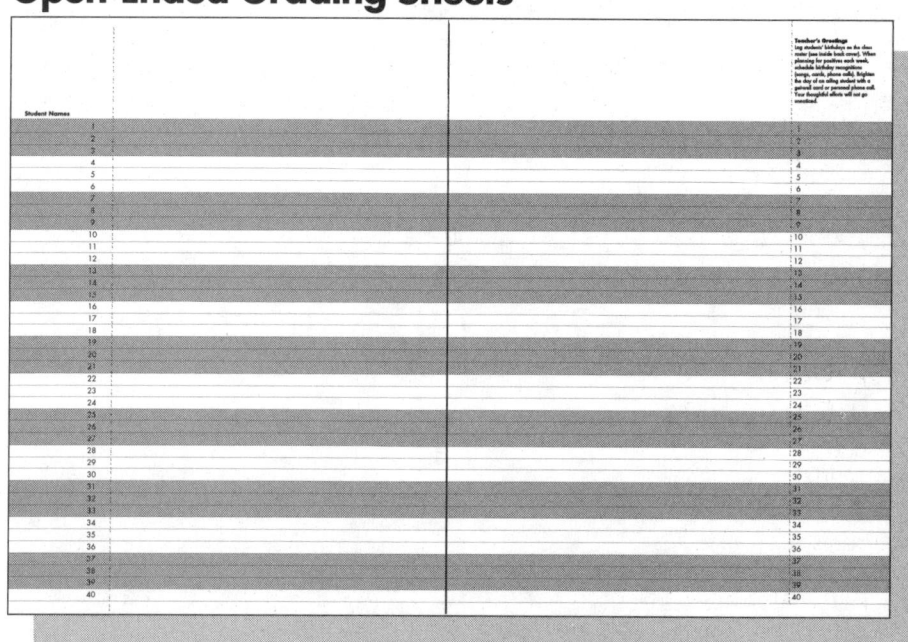

Teacher Tips. . . at Your Fingertips!

Look for terrific teacher tips that will ignite parent involvement, take the hassle out of homework, and provide classroom management ideas to help reduce academic and behavior problems.

Suggested Uses for Traditional Grading Sheets

1 Academic Grades

Record letter grades, numbers, percentages, checks and other marks to represent levels of mastery, achievement, improvement, proficiency, or development of skills.

Subject **MATH**

Student Names		Review (+) 9/8	P. 4 Prob. Sol. 9/10	Wrd. Problems 9/11	Time Test (+) 9/12	Review (-) 9/15	P. 7 Prob. Sol. 9/18
Chris	1	90	85	75	93	90	100
Nicole	2	95	95	90	100	90	95
Kenny	3	80	70	75	80	65	70
Robert	4	70	75	80	90	85	85
Stephanie	5	100	95	90	100	100	100
Leah	6	95	100	90	100	95	100
Danielle	7	100	100	90	100	95	90
Frank	8	100	100	95	85	90	95

2 Daily Accounting

Monitor items that are accounted for on a daily, weekly or periodic basis such as:

- homework completion,
- attendance,
- tokens or points earned, and
- citizenship grades.

Period *Literature - 4th Period*

	Winter Poem 1/5	Recitation 1/6	Choral Read. 1/7	Grammar Quiz 1/8	Book Report 1/9	Journal 1/12	Voc. Words 1/13	Voc. Sentences 1/14	Voc. Story 1/15	Voc. Test 1/16		
✓	✓	✓	✓	✓	✓	✓	✓	✓	✓		1 *Aaron*
✓	✓	Ⓧ	✓	✓	O	✓	✓	O			2 *Ricki*
✓	✓	✓	✓	✓	✓	✓	✓	✓	✓		3 *Kerri*
✓	Ⓧ	✓	✓	✓	✓	✓	✓	✓			4 *Ben*
✓	✓	✓	✓	✓	✓	✓	✓	✓			5 *Valerie*
AB	AB	✓	✓	✓	✓	✓	✓	✓			6 *Manuel*
✓	✓	✓	✓	✓	✓	✓	✓	✓			7 *Leticia*

Priority Overnight Messages Write "Priority Mail" on business-size envelopes and distribute to parents. Instruct them to use the envelopes to send in notes with their questions and concerns. Each morning ask students for "Priority Mail" envelopes. Respond immediately by note or phone.

3 Class Checklists

Keep track of miscellaneous replies or returns from students such as:

- permission slips,
- school forms,
- money collected (book orders, fund raisers, P.T.A. memberships), and
- R.S.V.P.'s.

Subject *Parent-signature replies*

Student Names		EMERGENCY FORM 9/5	LUNCH FORM 9/7	BEH. POLICY 9/10	H. WORK POLICY 9/11	P.T.A. Member. 9/12
Chris	1	✓	✓	✓	✓	✓
Nicole	2	✓	✓	✓	✓	✓
Kenny	3	✓	✓			
Robert	4	✓		✓	✓	✓
Stephanie	5	✓	✓		✓	
Leah	6	✓	✓	✓	✓	✓
Danielle	7		✓	✓	✓	✓
Frank	8	✓	✓	✓		
Jesse	9	✓	✓	✓	✓	✓
Levar	10	✓	✓	✓	✓	✓
Megan	11	✓	✓	✓	✓	✓
	12					

Suggested Uses for Open-Ended Grading Sheets

Written Evaluations

Perfect for jotting down notes concerning:

- a student's strengths.
- a student's weaknesses.
- new skills demonstrated by a student.
- progress in various proficiencies.

Essential for helping you key into areas that:

- need to be reviewed.
- need to be taught again.
- require assistance from an aide or specialist.

Great for portfolio assessments!

Student Names		Oral Book Report - November (Realistic Fiction)	Points
Chris	1	More confident - Good organization	90
Nicole	2	Well prepared - needs voice projection	85
Kenny	3	Great expression - descriptive lang.	95
Robert	4	Included creative analogies	90
Stephanie	5	One day late - few details - sketchy	70
Leah	6	Memorized favorite part - visuals	100
Danielle	7		
Frank	8		
Levar	9		
Megan	10		
Sheryl	11		
Tommy	12		
	13		
	14		
	15		

Evaluations in Progress

Assess a student's progress in a particular proficiency (i.e. writing) during the marking period by following these simple steps:

1 Create a horizontal space at the top of the sheet. Label the assessment criterion.

2 Divide the grid into thirds (vertically) and label with the assignment description and date. (You can also list several criteria to assess in each work sample.)

3 Collect three work samples over the course of the marking period. Record grades or comments.

See progress at a glance!

support 2=some evidence 3=good evidence 4=outstanding

SAMPLE #4 12/18		WRITING SAMPLE #5 1/30			WRITING SAMPLE #6 2/27			
Uses capitals correctly	Uses punctuation correctly	Expresses ideas clearly	Uses capitals correctly	Uses punctuation correctly	Expresses ideas clearly	Uses capitals correctly	Uses punctuation correctly	
3	2	3	4	4	4	4	3	1 Chris
2	2	2	2	2	3	3	3	2 Nicole
4	3	4	4	3	4	4	4	3 Kenny
3	2	3	3	3	3	4	4	4 Robert
2	2	3	3	2	3	3	3	5 Stephanie
3	3	4	4	3	4	4	4	6 Leah
2	2	3	3	2	3	3	3	7 Frank
								8
								9
								10
								11
								12
								13
								14
								15
								16
								17
								18
								19
								20

Clearing Up the Confusion

Many parents are confused abo[ut] how they can be involved in the[ir] children's education. The messa[ge] is clear: *Don't hesitate to comm[uni]cate.* Urge parents to phone or w[rite] whenever they have concerns. Assure them that their questions [are] important to you and to the succe[ss] of their children.

Combine Grades and Comments

Create an assessment tool that combines grades and comments.

- Combine **report grades** with specific comments about strengths and weaknesses.

- Combine **project grades** with notes regarding an exceptional performance.

- Combine math **test scores** with notes about areas that need to be reviewed or taught again.

Multi-Purpose Assignments

Assessing student proficiency in several areas within one assignment is as easy as 1...2...3!

1 Draw lines to create columns for recording grades or comments (each with a different assessment focus).

2 Indicate assignment and label columns.

3 Record grades and comments.

Cooperative Learning-Group Evaluations

Simplify cooperative learning-group evaluations using the open-ended sheets. Follow these steps:

1 List group members' names.

2 Assess the group as a whole, or assess individual group members in various areas:

- Performance of a task

- Understanding a concept

- Application of skills

- Cooperative behaviors

Form 1: Social Studies Project

Social Studies Project: Southwest Indians December 2–16th

Comment	Grade		Name
Lots of extra research	A	1	Chris
Good organization - too brief	B-	2	Nicole
Well prepared - creative	A-	3	Kenny
Much better descriptions	B+	4	Robert
Unorganized, few details	C-	5	Stephanie
Interesting facts/drawings	A	6	Leah
Big improvement - Good research	A	7	Danielle
		8	
		9	
		10	

Form 2: Current Events Oral Presentation

Current Events Oral Presentation week of 4/14

Student Names		Content	Comprehension	Presentation	
Aaron	1	ECONOMY B	B	B	
Ricki	2	HOMELESS A	A	A	
Heidi	3	ECONOMY A	C	B	
Ben	4	SCIENCE B	A	A	
Valerie	5	POLITICS A	C	B	
Manuel	6	HURRICANE A	A	A	
Leticia	7				
Cindy	8				
Darren	9				
Jason	10				
Jenni	11				
Carol	12				
Dirk	13				
	14				
	15				

Form 3: Cooperative Group Activity

ACTIVITY COOPERATIVE GROUP ACTIVITY "PET SURVEY"

FINAL PRODUCT	GROUP MEMBERS	INDIVIDUAL EFFORT	FINAL PRODUCT	
	Chris	10		1
	Robert	7		2
	Stephanie	9		3
8	Leticia	10	9	4
•organized	Manuel	8	•on time	5
•excellent	Hoang	9	•followed	6
visual	Phoebe	10	directions	7
aids	Jerry	8	• neat	8
				9

Subject_____

Student Names	ASSIGNMENT OR TEST	DATE																	
1																			
2																			
3																			
4																			
5																			
6																			
7																			
8																			
9																			
10																			
11																			
12																			
13																			
14																			
15																			
16																			
17																			
18																			
19																			
20																			
21																			
22																			
23																			
24																			
25																			
26																			
27																			
28																			
29																			
30																			
31																			
32																			
33																			
34																			
35																			
36																			
37																			
38																			
39																			
40																			

Subject

DATE

ASSIGNMENT OR TEST

Record-Breaking Attendance
Appeal to the "senses" and Back-to-School Night attendance will soar. Have parents sit at their child's desk to get a "feel" for the classroom. Present a feast for ears and eyes with a video presentation of a typical school day. Conclude the evening with delicious treats made by students.

1	
2	
3	
4	
5	
6	
7	
8	
9	
10	
11	
12	
13	
14	
15	
16	
17	
18	
19	
20	
21	
22	
23	
24	
25	
26	
27	
28	
29	
30	
31	
32	
33	
34	
35	
36	
37	
38	
39	
40	

Subject_____

Student Names	ASSIGNMENT OR TEST	DATE																		
1																				
2																				
3																				
4																				
5																				
6																				
7																				
8																				
9																				
10																				
11																				
12																				
13																				
14																				
15																				
16																				
17																				
18																				
19																				
20																				
21																				
22																				
23																				
24																				
25																				
26																				
27																				
28																				
29																				
30																				
31																				
32																				
33																				
34																				
35																				
36																				
37																				
38																				
39																				
40																				

Period _____

Parent Packets

Not all parents can attend Back-to-School Night, but all *do* need the information given. Send absentee parents a packet that includes an outline of your presentation, your discipline and homework policies, homework tips and other pertinent information. Make follow-up phone calls to answer any questions.

DATE	ASSIGNMENT OR TEST
	1
	2
	3
	4
	5
	6
	7
	8
	9
	10
	11
	12
	13
	14
	15
	16
	17
	18
	19
	20
	21
	22
	23
	24
	25
	26
	27
	28
	29
	30
	31
	32
	33
	34
	35
	36
	37
	38
	39
	40

Student Names	ASSIGNMENT OR TEST	DATE																		
1																				
2																				
3																				
4																				
5																				
6																				
7																				
8																				
9																				
10																				
11																				
12																				
13																				
14																				
15																				
16																				
17																				
18																				
19																				
20																				
21																				
22																				
23																				
24																				
25																				
26																				
27																				
28																				
29																				
30																				
31																				
32																				
33																				
34																				
35																				
36																				
37																				
38																				
39																				
40																				

DATE

ASSIGNMENT OR TEST

Great Expectations
Parents can't support your expectations if they don't know what they are. Clearly explain your discipline and homework expectations to parents at Back-to-School Night. Encourage questions and address any concerns. Send home a copy of these policies for parents to review with their children.

| 1 |
| 2 |
| 3 |
| 4 |
| 5 |
| 6 |
| 7 |
| 8 |
| 9 |
| 10 |
| 11 |
| 12 |
| 13 |
| 14 |
| 15 |
| 16 |
| 17 |
| 18 |
| 19 |
| 20 |
| 21 |
| 22 |
| 23 |
| 24 |
| 25 |
| 26 |
| 27 |
| 28 |
| 29 |
| 30 |
| 31 |
| 32 |
| 33 |
| 34 |
| 35 |
| 36 |
| 37 |
| 38 |
| 39 |
| 40 |

Subject_____

Student Names

	ASSIGNMENT OR TEST	DATE
1		
2		
3		
4		
5		
6		
7		
8		
9		
10		
11		
12		
13		
14		
15		
16		
17		
18		
19		
20		
21		
22		
23		
24		
25		
26		
27		
28		
29		
30		
31		
32		
33		
34		
35		
36		
37		
38		
39		
40		

Subject

Period _____

Planning for Positives

While planning your week's lessons, jot down the names of parents with whom you want to make positive contact during the upcoming week. Scheduling will make it happen. Keep track of completed phone calls and notes by transferring the information to the Parent Communication Logs on pages 159 and 160.

#
1
2
3
4
5
6
7
8
9
10
11
12
13
14
15
16
17
18
19
20
21
22
23
24
25
26
27
28
29
30
31
32
33
34
35
36
37
38
39
40

Subject

Student Names		DATE																														
		ASSIGNMENT OR TEST																														
	1																															
	2																															
	3																															
	4																															
	5																															
	6																															
	7																															
	8																															
	9																															
	10																															
	11																															
	12																															
	13																															
	14																															
	15																															
	16																															
	17																															
	18																															
	19																															
	20																															
	21																															
	22																															
	23																															
	24																															
	25																															
	26																															
	27																															
	28																															
	29																															
	30																															
	31																															
	32																															
	33																															
	34																															
	35																															
	36																															
	37																															
	38																															
	39																															
	40																															

Subject

Period _____

	DATE	
ASSIGNMENT OR TEST		
		1
		2
		3
		4
		5
		6
		7
		8
		9
		10
		11
		12
		13
		14
		15
		16
		17
		18
		19
		20
		21
		22
		23
		24
		25
		26
		27
		28
		29
		30
		31
		32
		33
		34
		35
		36
		37
		38
		39
		40

A New Look at Parent Conferences

A parent conference is a chance to do more than report student progress—it's a chance to set goals with parents, enlist their support, and make action plans to help ensure their child's success in school. See specific guidelines for regularly scheduled conferences on pages 149–150.

Student Names		DATE																					
		ASSIGNMENT OR TEST																					
	1																						
	2																						
	3																						
	4																						
	5																						
	6																						
	7																						
	8																						
	9																						
	10																						
	11																						
	12																						
	13																						
	14																						
	15																						
	16																						
	17																						
	18																						
	19																						
	20																						
	21																						
	22																						
	23																						
	24																						
	25																						
	26																						
	27																						
	28																						
	29																						
	30																						
	31																						
	32																						
	33																						
	34																						
	35																						
	36																						
	37																						
	38																						
	39																						
	40																						

Period _____

DATE

ASSIGNMENT OR TEST

	1
	2
	3
	4
	5
	6
	7
	8
	9
	10
	11
	12
	13
	14
	15
	16
	17
	18
	19
	20
	21
	22
	23
	24
	25
	26
	27
	28
	29
	30
	31
	32
	33
	34
	35
	36
	37
	38
	39
	40

Student Names		DATE																	
		ASSIGNMENT OR TEST																	
	1																		
	2																		
	3																		
	4																		
	5																		
	6																		
	7																		
	8																		
	9																		
	10																		
	11																		
	12																		
	13																		
	14																		
	15																		
	16																		
	17																		
	18																		
	19																		
	20																		
	21																		
	22																		
	23																		
	24																		
	25																		
	26																		
	27																		
	28																		
	29																		
	30																		
	31																		
	32																		
	33																		
	34																		
	35																		
	36																		
	37																		
	38																		
	39																		
	40																		

Subject

Period_____

DATE

ASSIGNMENT OR TEST

Academic Thunderbolts and Behavior Bombshells
Don't surprise parents on report cards or at midterm parent conferences with disappointing (and totally unexpected) behavior or academic news. Contact parents at the first sign of a problem. The sooner you enlist their support, the easier it will be to resolve the problem.

1
2
3
4
5
6
7
8
9
10
11
12
13
14
15
16
17
18
19
20
21
22
23
24
25
26
27
28
29
30
31
32
33
34
35
36
37
38
39
40

Subject

Student Names		DATE																													
		ASSIGNMENT OR TEST																														
	1																															
	2																															
	3																															
	4																															
	5																															
	6																															
	7																															
	8																															
	9																															
	10																															
	11																															
	12																															
	13																															
	14																															
	15																															
	16																															
	17																															
	18																															
	19																															
	20																															
	21																															
	22																															
	23																															
	24																															
	25																															
	26																															
	27																															
	28																															
	29																															
	30																															
	31																															
	32																															
	33																															
	34																															
	35																															
	36																															
	37																															
	38																															
	39																															
	40																															

DATE

ASSIGNMENT OR TEST

Try a Little T.L.C.
You want the best for your students, but you can't do it alone. Reach out to parents with a little T.L.C. (**t**eacher **l**aunched **c**ommunication). Fuel your communication efforts with phone calls, notes and conferences. Keep them going all year long with the specific parent communication resources on pages 147–160.

1
2
3
4
5
6
7
8
9
10
11
12
13
14
15
16
17
18
19
20
21
22
23
24
25
26
27
28
29
30
31
32
33
34
35
36
37
38
39
40

Period

Subject _____

Student Names		DATE																								
		ASSIGNMENT OR TEST																								
	1																									
	2																									
	3																									
	4																									
	5																									
	6																									
	7																									
	8																									
	9																									
	10																									
	11																									
	12																									
	13																									
	14																									
	15																									
	16																									
	17																									
	18																									
	19																									
	20																									
	21																									
	22																									
	23																									
	24																									
	25																									
	26																									
	27																									
	28																									
	29																									
	30																									
	31																									
	32																									
	33																									
	34																									
	35																									
	36																									
	37																									
	38																									
	39																									
	40																									

DATE

ASSIGNMENT OR TEST

"I Think There's a Problem"
Homework is the daily link between home and school. Encourage parents to contact you if: the homework seems either too easy or too difficult, more than the designated time is needed to complete homework, or the rationale for an assignment is unclear.

1
2
3
4
5
6
7
8
9
10
11
12
13
14
15
16
17
18
19
20
21
22
23
24
25
26
27
28
29
30
31
32
33
34
35
36
37
38
39
40

Period

Subject

Student Names	ASSIGNMENT OR TEST	DATE																																	
	1																																			
	2																																			
	3																																			
	4																																			
	5																																			
	6																																			
	7																																			
	8																																			
	9																																			
	10																																			
	11																																			
	12																																			
	13																																			
	14																																			
	15																																			
	16																																			
	17																																			
	18																																			
	19																																			
	20																																			
	21																																			
	22																																			
	23																																			
	24																																			
	25																																			
	26																																			
	27																																			
	28																																			
	29																																			
	30																																			
	31																																			
	32																																			
	33																																			
	34																																			
	35																																			
	36																																			
	37																																			
	38																																			
	39																																			
	40																																			

	DATE	ASSIGNMENT OR TEST

The Parent Involvement Test
When should you involve parents in school problems? The answer is simple. Contact parents at the first sign of a problem. Show students that school and home are united in working toward a successful solution to any problem. Still confused? Use the "Your Own Child" test on page 151.

#
1
2
3
4
5
6
7
8
9
10
11
12
13
14
15
16
17
18
19
20
21
22
23
24
25
26
27
28
29
30
31
32
33
34
35
36
37
38
39
40

Student Names	ASSIGNMENT OR TEST	DATE	Subject
	1		
	2		
	3		
	4		
	5		
	6		
	7		
	8		
	9		
	10		
	11		
	12		
	13		
	14		
	15		
	16		
	17		
	18		
	19		
	20		
	21		
	22		
	23		
	24		
	25		
	26		
	27		
	28		
	29		
	30		
	31		
	32		
	33		
	34		
	35		
	36		
	37		
	38		
	39		
	40		

Period

Getting Your Message Across—In Every Language!
Many of today's classrooms are filled with students whose families are new to this country. You need their support, too. Have translators (or older siblings) assist you with positive notes, phone calls, school correspondence and conferences.

1
2
3
4
5
6
7
8
9
10
11
12
13
14
15
16
17
18
19
20
21
22
23
24
25
26
27
28
29
30
31
32
33
34
35
36
37
38
39
40

Subject _____

Student Names		DATE / ASSIGNMENT OR TEST																											
	1																													
	2																													
	3																													
	4																													
	5																													
	6																													
	7																													
	8																													
	9																													
	10																													
	11																													
	12																													
	13																													
	14																													
	15																													
	16																													
	17																													
	18																													
	19																													
	20																													
	21																													
	22																													
	23																													
	24																													
	25																													
	26																													
	27																													
	28																													
	29																													
	30																													
	31																													
	32																													
	33																													
	34																													
	35																													
	36																													
	37																													
	38																													
	39																													
	40																													

Period _____

DATE

ASSIGNMENT OR TEST

Refrigerator Reminders
It's a cold fact, but homework time is often relegated to whenever it can be squeezed into a busy schedule. Advise parents to designate one evening as "homework scheduling" night. Suggest that the schedule be posted on the refrigerator as a "cool reminder" of homework time.

| 1 |
| 2 |
| 3 |
| 4 |
| 5 |
| 6 |
| 7 |
| 8 |
| 9 |
| 10 |
| 11 |
| 12 |
| 13 |
| 14 |
| 15 |
| 16 |
| 17 |
| 18 |
| 19 |
| 20 |
| 21 |
| 22 |
| 23 |
| 24 |
| 25 |
| 26 |
| 27 |
| 28 |
| 29 |
| 30 |
| 31 |
| 32 |
| 33 |
| 34 |
| 35 |
| 36 |
| 37 |
| 38 |
| 39 |
| 40 |

Subject _____

Student Names	ASSIGNMENT OR TEST	DATE																						
1																									
2																									
3																									
4																									
5																									
6																									
7																									
8																									
9																									
10																									
11																									
12																									
13																									
14																									
15																									
16																									
17																									
18																									
19																									
20																									
21																									
22																									
23																									
24																									
25																									
26																									
27																									
28																									
29																									
30																									
31																									
32																									
33																									
34																									
35																									
36																									
37																									
38																									
39																									
40																									

Period _____

ASSIGNMENT OR TEST

DATE

Terrific, Specific Praise
Demonstrate verbal praise techniques to parents during parent conferences. Explain that to be meaningful, praise must be specific. "Way to go" is not as meaningful as "This math test score is ten points higher than last time. Your flashcard game really helped. I'm very proud of you."

#
1
2
3
4
5
6
7
8
9
10
11
12
13
14
15
16
17
18
19
20
21
22
23
24
25
26
27
28
29
30
31
32
33
34
35
36
37
38
39
40

Subject _____

Student Names		DATE																				
		ASSIGNMENT OR TEST																				
	1																					
	2																					
	3																					
	4																					
	5																					
	6																					
	7																					
	8																					
	9																					
	10																					
	11																					
	12																					
	13																					
	14																					
	15																					
	16																					
	17																					
	18																					
	19																					
	20																					
	21																					
	22																					
	23																					
	24																					
	25																					
	26																					
	27																					
	28																					
	29																					
	30																					
	31																					
	32																					
	33																					
	34																					
	35																					
	36																					
	37																					
	38																					
	39																					
	40																					

Subject _____

Period _____

ASSIGNMENT OR TEST

Smooth Sailing for Transfer Students

Make a new student's transition easier with these welcome-wagon techniques: • Assign a "first-week friend" to the new student. • Send home your discipline plan and homework policy. • Place a phone call to the new student's parents, answering their questions about classroom or school policies.

	1
	2
	3
	4
	5
	6
	7
	8
	9
	10
	11
	12
	13
	14
	15
	16
	17
	18
	19
	20
	21
	22
	23
	24
	25
	26
	27
	28
	29
	30
	31
	32
	33
	34
	35
	36
	37
	38
	39
	40

Period _____

Subject _____

Student Names	DATE / ASSIGNMENT OR TEST																	
1																		
2																		
3																		
4																		
5																		
6																		
7																		
8																		
9																		
10																		
11																		
12																		
13																		
14																		
15																		
16																		
17																		
18																		
19																		
20																		
21																		
22																		
23																		
24																		
25																		
26																		
27																		
28																		
29																		
30																		
31																		
32																		
33																		
34																		
35																		
36																		
37																		
38																		
39																		
40																		

Period

DATE

ASSIGNMENT OR TEST

The "Appreciation" Hotline
Supportive parents will be especially grateful to receive a heartfelt thank you from the principal! Each month forward a "parent appreciation" list to your principal who then phones or writes to these parents expressing appreciation for the positive support they have given.

	DATE	ASSIGNMENT OR TEST
		1
		2
		3
		4
		5
		6
		7
		8
		9
		10
		11
		12
		13
		14
		15
		16
		17
		18
		19
		20
		21
		22
		23
		24
		25
		26
		27
		28
		29
		30
		31
		32
		33
		34
		35
		36
		37
		38
		39
		40

Period

Subject _____

Student Names		DATE																												
		ASSIGNMENT OR TEST																												
	1																													
	2																													
	3																													
	4																													
	5																													
	6																													
	7																													
	8																													
	9																													
	10																													
	11																													
	12																													
	13																													
	14																													
	15																													
	16																													
	17																													
	18																													
	19																													
	20																													
	21																													
	22																													
	23																													
	24																													
	25																													
	26																													
	27																													
	28																													
	29																													
	30																													
	31																													
	32																													
	33																													
	34																													
	35																													
	36																													
	37																													
	38																													
	39																													
	40																													

Subject _____

DATE

Period

Seeking Advice from the Experts

Who best understands a student's fears and faults, aspirations and crowning achievements? Parents, of course! Go right to parents for expert advice and valuable insights when problems arise at school. See Section Three for parent communication guidelines.

DATE

ASSIGNMENT OR TEST

	1
	2
	3
	4
	5
	6
	7
	8
	9
	10
	11
	12
	13
	14
	15
	16
	17
	18
	19
	20
	21
	22
	23
	24
	25
	26
	27
	28
	29
	30
	31
	32
	33
	34
	35
	36
	37
	38
	39
	40

Period

Student Names	DATE / ASSIGNMENT OR TEST																								
	1																								
	2																								
	3																								
	4																								
	5																								
	6																								
	7																								
	8																								
	9																								
	10																								
	11																								
	12																								
	13																								
	14																								
	15																								
	16																								
	17																								
	18																								
	19																								
	20																								
	21																								
	22																								
	23																								
	24																								
	25																								
	26																								
	27																								
	28																								
	29																								
	30																								
	31																								
	32																								
	33																								
	34																								
	35																								
	36																								
	37																								
	38																								
	39																								
	40																								

Period _____

DATE

ASSIGNMENT OR TEST

Pulling Together with Parents
Need support and follow-through from parents when problems arise? At conference time ask parents what tangible rewards or consequences work best at home to motivate their child. List them on a sheet of paper. Suggest that parents use this list when following up on positive or problem behavior at school.

	1
	2
	3
	4
	5
	6
	7
	8
	9
	10
	11
	12
	13
	14
	15
	16
	17
	18
	19
	20
	21
	22
	23
	24
	25
	26
	27
	28
	29
	30
	31
	32
	33
	34
	35
	36
	37
	38
	39
	40

Student Names		DATE																								
		ASSIGNMENT OR TEST																								
	1																									
	2																									
	3																									
	4																									
	5																									
	6																									
	7																									
	8																									
	9																									
	10																									
	11																									
	12																									
	13																									
	14																									
	15																									
	16																									
	17																									
	18																									
	19																									
	20																									
	21																									
	22																									
	23																									
	24																									
	25																									
	26																									
	27																									
	28																									
	29																									
	30																									
	31																									
	32																									
	33																									
	34																									
	35																									
	36																									
	37																									
	38																									
	39																									
	40																									

Period

	DATE	ASSIGNMENT OR TEST

Duty Calls

Contacting parents with concerns about a student's behavior or academic progress is a teacher's professional duty. A doctor wouldn't hesitate to call a parent about a child's medical problem. A concerned teacher is as much appreciated as a vigilant physician. Make that phone call for the support you need.

1	
2	
3	
4	
5	
6	
7	
8	
9	
10	
11	
12	
13	
14	
15	
16	
17	
18	
19	
20	
21	
22	
23	
24	
25	
26	
27	
28	
29	
30	
31	
32	
33	
34	
35	
36	
37	
38	
39	
40	

Period

Subject

Student Names	DATE / ASSIGNMENT OR TEST																			
1																				
2																				
3																				
4																				
5																				
6																				
7																				
8																				
9																				
10																				
11																				
12																				
13																				
14																				
15																				
16																				
17																				
18																				
19																				
20																				
21																				
22																				
23																				
24																				
25																				
26																				
27																				
28																				
29																				
30																				
31																				
32																				
33																				
34																				
35																				
36																				
37																				
38																				
39																				
40																				

Period _____

	DATE	ASSIGNMENT OR TEST

Parents and BIG Projects
Long-term reports and projects often require parent involvement. To help parents keep their children on track: • send home a detailed description of the project, • provide due dates for each stage of the project (outline, first draft, final copy), and • have parents sign-off each section as completed.

DATE	ASSIGNMENT OR TEST
	1
	2
	3
	4
	5
	6
	7
	8
	9
	10
	11
	12
	13
	14
	15
	16
	17
	18
	19
	20
	21
	22
	23
	24
	25
	26
	27
	28
	29
	30
	31
	32
	33
	34
	35
	36
	37
	38
	39
	40

Period

Student Names		DATE																						
		ASSIGNMENT OR TEST																						
	1																							
	2																							
	3																							
	4																							
	5																							
	6																							
	7																							
	8																							
	9																							
	10																							
	11																							
	12																							
	13																							
	14																							
	15																							
	16																							
	17																							
	18																							
	19																							
	20																							
	21																							
	22																							
	23																							
	24																							
	25																							
	26																							
	27																							
	28																							
	29																							
	30																							
	31																							
	32																							
	33																							
	34																							
	35																							
	36																							
	37																							
	38		DATE																						
	39		ASSIGNMENT OR TEST																						
	40																							

Period _____

ASSIGNMENT OR TEST

DATE

1
2
3
4
5
6
7
8
9
10
11
12
13
14
15
16
17
18
19
20
21
22
23
24
25
26
27
28
29
30
31
32
33
34
35
36
37
38
39
40

Period

Subject

Student Names		DATE / ASSIGNMENT OR TEST																										
	1																											
	2																											
	3																											
	4																											
	5																											
	6																											
	7																											
	8																											
	9																											
	10																											
	11																											
	12																											
	13																											
	14																											
	15																											
	16																											
	17																											
	18																											
	19																											
	20																											
	21																											
	22																											
	23																											
	24																											
	25																											
	26																											
	27																											
	28																											
	29																											
	30																											
	31																											
	32																											
	33																											
	34																											
	35																											
	36																											
	37																											
	38																											
	39																											
	40																											

Subject

Period _____

ASSIGNMENT OR TEST

Begin on a Positive Note
Share good news before problems
have a chance to start. Each student
excels at something. Find it and
share it. During the first weeks of
school, contact parents to relate
specific examples of good work
habits, athletic or artistic talents, or
positive attitudes. See Positive
Communication p. 148.

	1
	2
	3
	4
	5
	6
	7
	8
	9
	10
	11
	12
	13
	14
	15
	16
	17
	18
	19
	20
	21
	22
	23
	24
	25
	26
	27
	28
	29
	30
	31
	32
	33
	34
	35
	36
	37
	38
	39
	40

Period

Subject_____

Student Names	DATE ASSIGNMENT OR TEST																									
1																										
2																										
3																										
4																										
5																										
6																										
7																										
8																										
9																										
10																										
11																										
12																										
13																										
14																										
15																										
16																										
17																										
18																										
19																										
20																										
21																										
22																										
23																										
24																										
25																										
26																										
27																										
28																										
29																										
30																										
31																										
32																										
33																										
34																										
35																										
36																										
37																										
38																										
39																										
40																										

Period _____

DATE	ASSIGNMENT OR TEST
	1
	2
	3
	4
	5
	6
	7
	8
	9
	10
	11
	12
	13
	14
	15
	16
	17
	18
	19
	20
	21
	22
	23
	24
	25
	26
	27
	28
	29
	30
	31
	32
	33
	34
	35
	36
	37
	38
	39
	40

Period

Student Names		DATE																							
		ASSIGNMENT OR TEST																							
	1																								
	2																								
	3																								
	4																								
	5																								
	6																								
	7																								
	8																								
	9																								
	10																								
	11																								
	12																								
	13																								
	14																								
	15																								
	16																								
	17																								
	18																								
	19																								
	20																								
	21																								
	22																								
	23																								
	24																								
	25																								
	26																								
	27																								
	28																								
	29																								
	30																								
	31																								
	32																								
	33																								
	34																								
	35																								
	36																								
	37																								
	38																								
	39																								
	40																								

DATE

ASSIGNMENT OR TEST

Yellow Flags

As you record homework grades in your *Record Book Plus*, keep a watchful eye for sudden grade changes or incidences of incomplete, late or missing assignments. Highlight changes with a yellow marker. A student with two yellow marks needs your help. Enlist parent support with a phone call or note.

1
2
3
4
5
6
7
8
9
10
11
12
13
14
15
16
17
18
19
20
21
22
23
24
25
26
27
28
29
30
31
32
33
34
35
36
37
38
39
40

Period

Subject _____

Student Names	ASSIGNMENT OR TEST																							
DATE																								
1																								
2																								
3																								
4																								
5																								
6																								
7																								
8																								
9																								
10																								
11																								
12																								
13																								
14																								
15																								
16																								
17																								
18																								
19																								
20																								
21																								
22																								
23																								
24																								
25																								
26																								
27																								
28																								
29																								
30																								
31																								
32																								
33																								
34																								
35																								
36																								
37																								
38																								
39																								
40																								

Period_____

ASSIGNMENT OR TEST

Keeping a Handle on Homework
Ever hear this: "I did my homework, but I left it at home?" Time to get parents involved! Suggest that they discuss with their child an appropriate spot to place completed work each night. Encourage parents to praise their child when homework is retrieved from the designated spot.

1		
2		
3		
4		
5		
6		
7		
8		
9		
10		
11		
12		
13		
14		
15		
16		
17		
18		
19		
20		
21		
22		
23		
24		
25		
26		
27		
28		
29		
30		
31		
32		
33		
34		
35		
36		
37		
38		
39		
40		

Period_____

Subject

Student Names		DATE																													
		ASSIGNMENT OR TEST																													
	1																														
	2																														
	3																														
	4																														
	5																														
	6																														
	7																														
	8																														
	9																														
	10																														
	11																														
	12																														
	13																														
	14																														
	15																														
	16																														
	17																														
	18																														
	19																														
	20																														
	21																														
	22																														
	23																														
	24																														
	25																														
	26																														
	27																														
	28																														
	29																														
	30																														
	31																														
	32																														
	33																														
	34																														
	35																														
	36																														
	37																														
	38																														
	39																														
	40																														

Subject

DATE

Period _____

DATE

ASSIGNMENT OR TEST

Priority Overnight Messages
Write "Priority Mail" on business-size envelopes and distribute to parents. Instruct them to use the envelopes to send in notes with their questions and concerns. Each morning ask students for "Priority Mail" envelopes. Respond immediately by note or phone.

																#
																1
																2
																3
																4
																5
																6
																7
																8
																9
																10
																11
																12
																13
																14
																15
																16
																17
																18
																19
																20
																21
																22
																23
																24
																25
																26
																27
																28
																29
																30
																31
																32
																33
																34
																35
																36
																37
																38
																39
																40

Period

Student Names		DATE																										
		ASSIGNMENT OR TEST																										
	1																											
	2																											
	3																											
	4																											
	5																											
	6																											
	7																											
	8																											
	9																											
	10																											
	11																											
	12																											
	13																											
	14																											
	15																											
	16																											
	17																											
	18																											
	19																											
	20																											
	21																											
	22																											
	23																											
	24																											
	25																											
	26																											
	27																											
	28																											
	29																											
	30																											
	31																											
	32																											
	33																											
	34																											
	35																											
	36																											
	37																											
	38																											
	39																											
	40																											

Subject

Period_____

ASSIGNMENT OR TEST

Homework—Get It in Writing!
If parents are to encourage good homework habits, they need to know what homework is being given. All assignments must be written down— either copied by the student into a homework booklet or duplicated by you on a weekly homework sheet. Provide a parent sign-off space on all assignment sheets.

	1
	2
	3
	4
	5
	6
	7
	8
	9
	10
	11
	12
	13
	14
	15
	16
	17
	18
	19
	20
	21
	22
	23
	24
	25
	26
	27
	28
	29
	30
	31
	32
	33
	34
	35
	36
	37
	38
	39
	40

Subject _____

Student Names		DATE																														
		ASSIGNMENT OR TEST																															
1																																	
2																																	
3																																	
4																																	
5																																	
6																																	
7																																	
8																																	
9																																	
10																																	
11																																	
12																																	
13																																	
14																																	
15																																	
16																																	
17																																	
18																																	
19																																	
20																																	
21																																	
22																																	
23																																	
24																																	
25																																	
26																																	
27																																	
28																																	
29																																	
30																																	
31																																	
32																																	
33																																	
34																																	
35																																	
36																																	
37																																	
38																																	
39																																	
40																																	

Subject _____

Period_____

	DATE	ASSIGNMENT OR TEST

Coming Attractions!
Inform students and parents of upcoming tests and due dates with a "Coming Attractions" memo. Draw a movie marquee and fill it in with important information: "Coming Attraction—Math Test... Starring (student's name)... Produced by (teacher's name)... Coming on (test or due date)."

1
2
3
4
5
6
7
8
9
10
11
12
13
14
15
16
17
18
19
20
21
22
23
24
25
26
27
28
29
30
31
32
33
34
35
36
37
38
39
40

Student Names	DATE / ASSIGNMENT OR TEST																						
Subject																							
1																							
2																							
3																							
4																							
5																							
6																							
7																							
8																							
9																							
10																							
11																							
12																							
13																							
14																							
15																							
16																							
17																							
18																							
19																							
20																							
21																							
22																							
23																							
24																							
25																							
26																							
27																							
28																							
29																							
30																							
31																							
32																							
33																							
34																							
35																							
36																							
37																							
38																							
39																							
40																							

Period _____

DATE

ASSIGNMENT OR TEST

	1
	2
	3
	4
	5
	6
	7
	8
	9
	10
	11
	12
	13
	14
	15
	16
	17
	18
	19
	20
	21
	22
	23
	24
	25
	26
	27
	28
	29
	30
	31
	32
	33
	34
	35
	36
	37
	38
	39
	40

Subject _____

Student Names	ASSIGNMENT OR TEST	DATE																	
1																			
2																			
3																			
4																			
5																			
6																			
7																			
8																			
9																			
10																			
11																			
12																			
13																			
14																			
15																			
16																			
17																			
18																			
19																			
20																			
21																			
22																			
23																			
24																			
25																			
26																			
27																			
28																			
29																			
30																			
31																			
32																			
33																			
34																			
35																			
36																			
37																			
38																			
39																			
40																			

Period _____

DATE

ASSIGNMENT OR TEST

	1
	2
	3
	4
	5
	6
	7
	8
	9
	10
	11
	12
	13
	14
	15
	16
	17
	18
	19
	20
	21
	22
	23
	24
	25
	26
	27
	28
	29
	30
	31
	32
	33
	34
	35
	36
	37
	38
	39
	40

Subject _____

Student Names		DATE																							
		ASSIGNMENT OR TEST																							
	1																								
	2																								
	3																								
	4																								
	5																								
	6																								
	7																								
	8																								
	9																								
	10																								
	11																								
	12																								
	13																								
	14																								
	15																								
	16																								
	17																								
	18																								
	19																								
	20																								
	21																								
	22																								
	23																								
	24																								
	25																								
	26																								
	27																								
	28																								
	29																								
	30																								
	31																								
	32																								
	33																								
	34																								
	35																								
	36																								
	37																								
	38																								
	39																								
	40																								

Subject _____

Period _____

ASSIGNMENT OR TEST

Sharing Success Stories
When a struggling student passes a test, wins a race, or shows improvement in a challenging subject, immediately share that success by phoning parents or sending a note home. Just call and say, "I'd like to share a great success story with you!"

	DATE
1	
2	
3	
4	
5	
6	
7	
8	
9	
10	
11	
12	
13	
14	
15	
16	
17	
18	
19	
20	
21	
22	
23	
24	
25	
26	
27	
28	
29	
30	
31	
32	
33	
34	
35	
36	
37	
38	
39	
40	

Student Names

1	
2	
3	
4	
5	
6	
7	
8	
9	
10	
11	
12	
13	
14	
15	
16	
17	
18	
19	
20	
21	
22	
23	
24	
25	
26	
27	
28	
29	
30	
31	
32	
33	
34	
35	
36	
37	
38	
39	
40	

1
2
3
4
5
6
7
8
9
10
11
12
13
14
15
16
17
18
19
20
21
22
23
24
25
26
27
28
29
30
31
32
33
34
35
36
37
38
39
40

Student Names

1	
2	
3	
4	
5	
6	
7	
8	
9	
10	
11	
12	
13	
14	
15	
16	
17	
18	
19	
20	
21	
22	
23	
24	
25	
26	
27	
28	
29	
30	
31	
32	
33	
34	
35	
36	
37	
38	
39	
40	

Keeping Your Promises
A problem-solving conference should
end with your promise. Pledge to
update parents by phone or note on
a specific date, preferably within the
week. Don't break that promise. This
follow-up communication is
imperative to the success of your
problem-solving sessions and parent
support efforts.

1
2
3
4
5
6
7
8
9
10
11
12
13
14
15
16
17
18
19
20
21
22
23
24
25
26
27
28
29
30
31
32
33
34
35
36
37
38
39
40

Student Names

1	
2	
3	
4	
5	
6	
7	
8	
9	
10	
11	
12	
13	
14	
15	
16	
17	
18	
19	
20	
21	
22	
23	
24	
25	
26	
27	
28	
29	
30	
31	
32	
33	
34	
35	
36	
37	
38	
39	
40	

1
2
3
4
5
6
7
8
9
10
11
12
13
14
15
16
17
18
19
20
21
22
23
24
25
26
27
28
29
30
31
32
33
34
35
36
37
38
39
40

Student Names

1	
2	
3	
4	
5	
6	
7	
8	
9	
10	
11	
12	
13	
14	
15	
16	
17	
18	
19	
20	
21	
22	
23	
24	
25	
26	
27	
28	
29	
30	
31	
32	
33	
34	
35	
36	
37	
38	
39	
40	

1
2
3
4
5
6
7
8
9
10
11
12
13
14
15
16
17
18
19
20
21
22
23
24
25
26
27
28
29
30
31
32
33
34
35
36
37
38
39
40

Student Names

1	
2	
3	
4	
5	
6	
7	
8	
9	
10	
11	
12	
13	
14	
15	
16	
17	
18	
19	
20	
21	
22	
23	
24	
25	
26	
27	
28	
29	
30	
31	
32	
33	
34	
35	
36	
37	
38	
39	
40	

1
2
3
4
5
6
7
8
9
10
11
12
13
14
15
16
17
18
19
20
21
22
23
24
25
26
27
28
29
30
31
32
33
34
35
36
37
38
39
40

Student Names

	1
	2
	3
	4
	5
	6
	7
	8
	9
	10
	11
	12
	13
	14
	15
	16
	17
	18
	19
	20
	21
	22
	23
	24
	25
	26
	27
	28
	29
	30
	31
	32
	33
	34
	35
	36
	37
	38
	39
	40

Speed Up the Referral Process
Do you suspect a student needs special assistance from resource personnel? Speed up the referral process by keeping consistent, factual, dated documentation on the specially designed Behavior Documentation Sheets in Section Two. (See page 105 for more information.)

1

2

3

4

5

6

7

8

9

10

11

12

13

14

15

16

17

18

19

20

21

22

23

24

25

26

27

28

29

30

31

32

33

34

35

36

37

38

39

40

Student Names

1	
2	
3	
4	
5	
6	
7	
8	
9	
10	
11	
12	
13	
14	
15	
16	
17	
18	
19	
20	
21	
22	
23	
24	
25	
26	
27	
28	
29	
30	
31	
32	
33	
34	
35	
36	
37	
38	
39	
40	

It's Conference Time
When academic or behavior problems persist, despite actions you've taken at school, contact parents by phone to arrange a problem-solving conference. Briefly update the problem and set a convenient time to meet. See detailed guidelines in Section Three, pages 149-150.

1
2
3
4
5
6
7
8
9
10
11
12
13
14
15
16
17
18
19
20
21
22
23
24
25
26
27
28
29
30
31
32
33
34
35
36
37
38
39
40

Student Names

1	
2	
3	
4	
5	
6	
7	
8	
9	
10	
11	
12	
13	
14	
15	
16	
17	
18	
19	
20	
21	
22	
23	
24	
25	
26	
27	
28	
29	
30	
31	
32	
33	
34	
35	
36	
37	
38	
39	
40	

Handling Difficult Situations

If a parent becomes angry or upset during a phone call or conference, remain calm and follow these steps to "cool down" the situation:

1. Thank the parent for being concerned.
2. Ask for specific examples of the problem.
3. Identify the real issues.
4. Use the guidelines on pages 156–158 to solve the problem together.

1

2

3

4

5

6

7

8

9

10

11

12

13

14

15

16

17

18

19

20

21

22

23

24

25

26

27

28

29

30

31

32

33

34

35

36

37

38

39

40

Student Names

1	
2	
3	
4	
5	
6	
7	
8	
9	
10	
11	
12	
13	
14	
15	
16	
17	
18	
19	
20	
21	
22	
23	
24	
25	
26	
27	
28	
29	
30	
31	
32	
33	
34	
35	
36	
37	
38	
39	
40	

1

2

3

4

5

6

7

8

9

10

11

12

13

14

15

16

17

18

19

20

21

22

23

24

25

26

27

28

29

30

31

32

33

34

35

36

37

38

39

40

Student Names

1	
2	
3	
4	
5	
6	
7	
8	
9	
10	
11	
12	
13	
14	
15	
16	
17	
18	
19	
20	
21	
22	
23	
24	
25	
26	
27	
28	
29	
30	
31	
32	
33	
34	
35	
36	
37	
38	
39	
40	

1
2
3
4
5
6
7
8
9
10
11
12
13
14
15
16
17
18
19
20
21
22
23
24
25
26
27
28
29
30
31
32
33
34
35
36
37
38
39
40

Student Names

1	
2	
3	
4	
5	
6	
7	
8	
9	
10	
11	
12	
13	
14	
15	
16	
17	
18	
19	
20	
21	
22	
23	
24	
25	
26	
27	
28	
29	
30	
31	
32	
33	
34	
35	
36	
37	
38	
39	
40	

1

2

3

4

5

6

7

8

9

10

11

12

13

14

15

16

17

18

19

20

21

22

23

24

25

26

27

28

29

30

31

32

33

34

35

36

37

38

39

40

Student Names

1	
2	
3	
4	
5	
6	
7	
8	
9	
10	
11	
12	
13	
14	
15	
16	
17	
18	
19	
20	
21	
22	
23	
24	
25	
26	
27	
28	
29	
30	
31	
32	
33	
34	
35	
36	
37	
38	
39	
40	

	1
	2
	3
	4
	5
	6
	7
	8
	9
	10
	11
	12
	13
	14
	15
	16
	17
	18
	19
	20
	21
	22
	23
	24
	25
	26
	27
	28
	29
	30
	31
	32
	33
	34
	35
	36
	37
	38
	39
	40

Student Names

1	
2	
3	
4	
5	
6	
7	
8	
9	
10	
11	
12	
13	
14	
15	
16	
17	
18	
19	
20	
21	
22	
23	
24	
25	
26	
27	
28	
29	
30	
31	
32	
33	
34	
35	
36	
37	
38	
39	
40	

1
2
3
4
5
6
7
8
9
10
11
12
13
14
15
16
17
18
19
20
21
22
23
24
25
26
27
28
29
30
31
32
33
34
35
36
37
38
39
40

Student Names

1	
2	
3	
4	
5	
6	
7	
8	
9	
10	
11	
12	
13	
14	
15	
16	
17	
18	
19	
20	
21	
22	
23	
24	
25	
26	
27	
28	
29	
30	
31	
32	
33	
34	
35	
36	
37	
38	
39	
40	

1
2
3
4
5
6
7
8
9
10
11
12
13
14
15
16
17
18
19
20
21
22
23
24
25
26
27
28
29
30
31
32
33
34
35
36
37
38
39
40

Student Names

1	
2	
3	
4	
5	
6	
7	
8	
9	
10	
11	
12	
13	
14	
15	
16	
17	
18	
19	
20	
21	
22	
23	
24	
25	
26	
27	
28	
29	
30	
31	
32	
33	
34	
35	
36	
37	
38	
39	
40	

Side by Side
Problem-solving is a joint effort—
teacher and parents working together
to help the student. Weave the word
"we" into all your conversations and
communications. "We must work
together." "We can solve this
problem together." "We must support
each other." "We can make a
difference."

1

2

3

4

5

6

7

8

9

10

11

12

13

14

15

16

17

18

19

20

21

22

23

24

25

26

27

28

29

30

31

32

33

34

35

36

37

38

39

40

Student Names

	1
	2
	3
	4
	5
	6
	7
	8
	9
	10
	11
	12
	13
	14
	15
	16
	17
	18
	19
	20
	21
	22
	23
	24
	25
	26
	27
	28
	29
	30
	31
	32
	33
	34
	35
	36
	37
	38
	39
	40

BEHAVIOR DOCUMENTATION

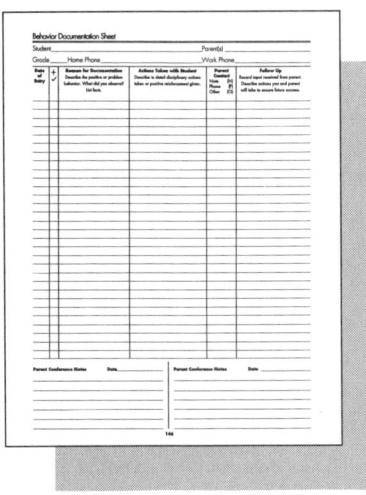

Behavior documentation will help you:

- Create an individual profile of a student's behavior at school.

- Provide the professional backup you need to communicate effectively with parents and to increase their support for your efforts.

- Gain administrative and resource support when thorough documentation is required in the referral process.

SECTION TWO

Behavior Documentation Sheets

The documentation you must have to get the
- Parent Support
- Administrative Support
- Resource Services

you and your students need!

Parent Support

Parents need to know about their children's ups and downs—academically and behaviorally. They need to know when a problem exists, how the problem is being handled, and what they can do to help. They also need to hear about their children's positive behavior so that those successes can be recognized and reinforced at home.

Accurate, dated, factual behavior documentation gives you the tools to confidently and professionally work with parents for the benefit of their children.

Administrative Support

Before getting involved in the behavior-management loop, your administrator needs to know the nature of a student's behavior problem, when it occurred, and what actions you have taken with the student (and parents) to solve the problem. Your objective reporting of a student's behavior (documented on the Behavior Documentation Sheet) will be invaluable in getting your administrator involved in the problem-solving process.

The positive behavior entries on the Behavior Documentation Sheets (i.e. outstanding behavior, noteworthy improvements, awards) should be shared with your administrator so that additional student recognition and parent communication can be provided on an administrative level.

Resource Services Support

Complete and factual data is essential for a student to qualify for resource services such as special education, speech and language, guidance counseling, and remedial reading. By using the Behavior Documentation Sheets to keep consistent, dated records of student performance and your attempts to deal with problems, you will speed up the referral process and get the help that your students need.

How to Use the Behavior Documentation Sheet

1 **Record the date of the problem or positive behavior.**

2 **Write a check mark (✓) to indicate a problem behavior or a plus (+) to indicate a positive entry.**

Always document the first sign of a problem and enlist the support of parents immediately. The sooner you address a behavior problem, the easier it will be to solve. When you are unsure about whether to contact a parent about a student's behavior, use the "Your Own Child" test on page 151.

Remember to document positive behavior, too, especially when it occurs within the problem-solving process. Give recognition to students to support their responsible behavior and communicate the good news to parents.

3 **Write a detailed description of the behavior.**

Be specific. Describe behavior in observable terms. (See sample below.) Avoid subjective

statements and vague opinions such as "She just won't listen," or "His behavior is getting worse and worse." Parents will be more receptive and willing to support you when you have given them an accurate record of what occurred.

4 **Describe in detail the actions you have taken with the student.**

For problem behavior, make specific notes about the disciplinary actions you have taken. For positive behavior, indicate the positive reinforcement and recognition you have given.

5 **Note the type of parent contact, if any, that was made.**

For parent communication resources, refer to Section Three, pages 147-160.

6 **Record follow-up actions to be taken by you and parents.**

Indicate steps you and parents will take, and a date for follow-up contact.

Behavior Documentation Sheet

Student _Megan Andrews_   Parent(s) _Tom & Sue Andrews_

Grade _2_ Home Phone _555-2417_   Work Phone _555-6710_

Date of Entry	+ / ✓	Reason for Documentation Describe the positive or problem behavior. What did you observe? List facts.	Actions Taken with Student Describe in detail disciplinary actions taken or positive reinforcement given.	Parent Contact Note (N) Phone (P) Other (O)	Follow Up Record input received from parent. Describe actions you and parent will take to ensure future success.
10·3	✓	Megan trips Joey during Math	Conference w/Megan. She apologizes to Joey.	None	
10·5	✓	Megan trips Susan & Bill during Reading.	Conference w/Megan. Writes apologies to Susan & Bill. Last in line all day.	P	Talk to Mother during lunch. Ask her to remind Megan about proper behavior. Mom will restrict T.V. if it happens again.

Behavior Documentation Sheet

Student_____ Parent(s) _____

Grade_____ Home Phone_____ Work Phone_____

Date of Entry	+ ✓	**Reason for Documentation** Describe the positive or problem behavior. What did you observe? List facts.	**Actions Taken with Student** Describe in detail disciplinary actions taken or positive reinforcement given.	**Parent Contact** Note (N) Phone (P) Other (O)	**Follow Up** Record input received from parent. Describe actions you and parent will take to ensure future success.

Parent Conference Notes   **Date**_____

_____

_____

_____

Parent Conference Notes   **Date** _____

_____

_____

_____

Behavior Documentation Sheet

Student _____ Parent(s) _____

Grade _____ Home Phone _____ Work Phone _____

Date of Entry	+ / ✓	**Reason for Documentation** Describe the positive or problem behavior. What did you observe? List facts.	**Actions Taken with Student** Describe in detail disciplinary actions taken or positive reinforcement given.	**Parent Contact** Note (N) Phone (P) Other (O)	**Follow Up** Record input received from parent. Describe actions you and parent will take to ensure future success.

Parent Conference Notes   Date _____

_____
_____
_____
_____

Parent Conference Notes   Date _____

_____
_____
_____
_____

Behavior Documentation Sheet

Student _____ Parent(s) _____

Grade _____ Home Phone _____ Work Phone _____

Date of Entry	+ / ✓	Reason for Documentation Describe the positive or problem behavior. What did you observe? List facts.	Actions Taken with Student Describe in detail disciplinary actions taken or positive reinforcement given.	Parent Contact Note (N) Phone (P) Other (O)	Follow Up Record input received from parent. Describe actions you and parent will take to ensure future success.

Parent Conference Notes   Date _____

_____

_____

_____

_____

Parent Conference Notes   Date _____

_____

_____

_____

_____

Behavior Documentation Sheet

Student _____ Parent(s) _____

Grade _____ Home Phone _____ Work Phone _____

Date of Entry	+ ✓	**Reason for Documentation** Describe the positive or problem behavior. What did you observe? List facts.	**Actions Taken with Student** Describe in detail disciplinary actions taken or positive reinforcement given.	**Parent Contact** Note (N) Phone (P) Other (O)	**Follow Up** Record input received from parent. Describe actions you and parent will take to ensure future success.

Parent Conference Notes   Date _____

Parent Conference Notes   Date _____

Behavior Documentation Sheet

Student_____ Parent(s) _____

Grade_____ Home Phone_____ Work Phone_____

Date of Entry	+ ✓	**Reason for Documentation** Describe the positive or problem behavior. What did you observe? List facts.	**Actions Taken with Student** Describe in detail disciplinary actions taken or positive reinforcement given.	**Parent Contact** Note (N) Phone (P) Other (O)	**Follow Up** Record input received from parent. Describe actions you and parent will take to ensure future success.

Parent Conference Notes   Date_____

_____

_____

_____

_____

Parent Conference Notes   Date _____

_____

_____

_____

_____

Behavior Documentation Sheet

Student_____ Parent(s)_____

Grade_____ Home Phone_____ Work Phone_____

Date of Entry	+ / ✓	**Reason for Documentation** Describe the positive or problem behavior. What did you observe? List facts.	**Actions Taken with Student** Describe in detail disciplinary actions taken or positive reinforcement given.	**Parent Contact** Note (N) Phone (P) Other (O)	**Follow Up** Record input received from parent. Describe actions you and parent will take to ensure future success.

Parent Conference Notes   **Date**_____

_____
_____
_____
_____

Parent Conference Notes   **Date**_____

_____
_____
_____
_____

Behavior Documentation Sheet

Student_____ Parent(s) _____

Grade _____ Home Phone _____ Work Phone _____

Date of Entry	+ ✓	Reason for Documentation Describe the positive or problem behavior. What did you observe? List facts.	Actions Taken with Student Describe in detail disciplinary actions taken or positive reinforcement given.	Parent Contact Note (N) Phone (P) Other (O)	Follow Up Record input received from parent. Describe actions you and parent will take to ensure future success.

Parent Conference Notes   Date_____

_____

_____

_____

_____

Parent Conference Notes   Date _____

_____

_____

_____

_____

Behavior Documentation Sheet

Student_____ Parent(s) _____

Grade _____ Home Phone _____ Work Phone _____

Date of Entry	+ ✓	**Reason for Documentation** Describe the positive or problem behavior. What did you observe? List facts.	**Actions Taken with Student** Describe in detail disciplinary actions taken or positive reinforcement given.	**Parent Contact** Note (N) Phone (P) Other (O)	**Follow Up** Record input received from parent. Describe actions you and parent will take to ensure future success.

Parent Conference Notes   Date _____

_____

_____

_____

_____

Parent Conference Notes   Date _____

_____

_____

_____

_____

Behavior Documentation Sheet

Student _____ Parent(s) _____

Grade _____ Home Phone _____ Work Phone _____

Date of Entry	+ ✓	Reason for Documentation Describe the positive or problem behavior. What did you observe? List facts.	Actions Taken with Student Describe in detail disciplinary actions taken or positive reinforcement given.	Parent Contact Note (N) Phone (P) Other (O)	Follow Up Record input received from parent. Describe actions you and parent will take to ensure future success.

Parent Conference Notes   **Date** _____

_____

_____

_____

_____

Parent Conference Notes   **Date** _____

_____

_____

_____

_____

Behavior Documentation Sheet

Student_____   Parent(s) _____

Grade_____Home Phone_____   Work Phone_____

Date of Entry	+ / ✓	Reason for Documentation Describe the positive or problem behavior. What did you observe? List facts.	Actions Taken with Student Describe in detail disciplinary actions taken or positive reinforcement given.	Parent Contact Note (N) Phone (P) Other (O)	Follow Up Record input received from parent. Describe actions you and parent will take to ensure future success.

Parent Conference Notes   Date _____

_____
_____
_____
_____
_____

Parent Conference Notes   Date _____

_____
_____
_____
_____
_____

Behavior Documentation Sheet

Student_____ Parent(s) _____

Grade _____ Home Phone _____ Work Phone _____

Date of Entry	+ ✓	**Reason for Documentation** Describe the positive or problem behavior. What did you observe? List facts.	**Actions Taken with Student** Describe in detail disciplinary actions taken or positive reinforcement given.	**Parent Contact** Note (N) Phone (P) Other (O)	**Follow Up** Record input received from parent. Describe actions you and parent will take to ensure future success.

Parent Conference Notes   Date_____

_____

_____

_____

_____

Parent Conference Notes   Date_____

_____

_____

_____

_____

Behavior Documentation Sheet

Student_____ Parent(s) _____

Grade_____ Home Phone_____ Work Phone_____

Date of Entry	+ ✓	Reason for Documentation Describe the positive or problem behavior. What did you observe? List facts.	Actions Taken with Student Describe in detail disciplinary actions taken or positive reinforcement given.	Parent Contact Note (N) Phone (P) Other (O)	Follow Up Record input received from parent. Describe actions you and parent will take to ensure future success.

Parent Conference Notes   Date _____

_____

_____

_____

_____

Parent Conference Notes   Date _____

_____

_____

_____

_____

Behavior Documentation Sheet

Student_____ Parent(s) _____

Grade_____ Home Phone_____ Work Phone_____

Date of Entry	+ / ✓	**Reason for Documentation** Describe the positive or problem behavior. What did you observe? List facts.	**Actions Taken with Student** Describe in detail disciplinary actions taken or positive reinforcement given.	**Parent Contact** Note (N) Phone (P) Other (O)	**Follow Up** Record input received from parent. Describe actions you and parent will take to ensure future success.

Parent Conference Notes   Date_____

_____

_____

_____

_____

Parent Conference Notes   Date_____

_____

_____

_____

_____

Behavior Documentation Sheet

Student_____ Parent(s) _____

Grade _____ Home Phone _____ Work Phone_____

Date & Entry	+ ✓	**Reason for Documentation** Describe the positive or problem behavior. What did you observe? List facts.	**Actions Taken with Student** Describe in detail disciplinary actions taken or positive reinforcement given.	**Parent Contact** Note (N) Phone (P) Other (O)	**Follow Up** Record input received from parent. Describe actions you and parent will take to ensure future success.

Parent Conference Notes   Date _____

_____
_____
_____
_____
_____

Parent Conference Notes   Date _____

_____
_____
_____
_____
_____

Behavior Documentation Sheet

Student_____ Parent(s) _____

Grade_____ Home Phone_____ Work Phone_____

Date of Entry	+ ✓	Reason for Documentation Describe the positive or problem behavior. What did you observe? List facts.	Actions Taken with Student Describe in detail disciplinary actions taken or positive reinforcement given.	Parent Contact Note (N) Phone (P) Other (O)	Follow Up Record input received from parent. Describe actions you and parent will take to ensure future success.

Parent Conference Notes   Date_____

_____

_____

_____

_____

Parent Conference Notes   Date_____

_____

_____

_____

_____

havior Documentation Sheet

dent_____ Parent(s) _____

ade_____ Home Phone_____ Work Phone_____

te of ry	+ / ✓	**Reason for Documentation** Describe the positive or problem behavior. What did you observe? List facts.	**Actions Taken with Student** Describe in detail disciplinary actions taken or positive reinforcement given.	**Parent Contact** Note (N) Phone (P) Other (O)	**Follow Up** Record input received from parent. Describe actions you and parent will take to ensure future success.

arent Conference Notes   Date _____   **Parent Conference Notes**   Date _____

_____   _____
_____   _____
_____   _____
_____   _____
_____   _____
_____   _____

Behavior Documentation Sheet

Student_____ Parent(s) _____

Grade_____ Home Phone_____ Work Phone_____

Date of Entry	+ ✓	Reason for Documentation Describe the positive or problem behavior. What did you observe? List facts.	Actions Taken with Student Describe in detail disciplinary actions taken or positive reinforcement given.	Parent Contact Note (N) Phone (P) Other (O)	Follow Up Record input received from parent. Describe actions you and parent will take to ensure future success.

Parent Conference Notes   **Date**_____

_____
_____
_____
_____
_____

Parent Conference Notes   **Date** _____

_____
_____
_____
_____
_____

Behavior Documentation Sheet

Student _____ Parent(s) _____

Grade _____ Home Phone _____ Work Phone _____

Date of Entry	+ / ✓	**Reason for Documentation** Describe the positive or problem behavior. What did you observe? List facts.	**Actions Taken with Student** Describe in detail disciplinary actions taken or positive reinforcement given.	**Parent Contact** Note (N) Phone (P) Other (O)	**Follow Up** Record input received from parent. Describe actions you and parent will take to ensure future success.

Parent Conference Notes   Date _____

_____
_____
_____
_____

Parent Conference Notes   Date _____

_____
_____
_____
_____

Behavior Documentation Sheet

Student_____ Parent(s) _____

Grade _____ Home Phone _____ Work Phone _____

Date of Entry	+ / ✓	**Reason for Documentation** Describe the positive or problem behavior. What did you observe? List facts.	**Actions Taken with Student** Describe in detail disciplinary actions taken or positive reinforcement given.	**Parent Contact** Note (N) Phone (P) Other (O)	**Follow Up** Record input received from parent. Describe actions you and parent will take to ensure future success.

Parent Conference Notes   Date_____

_____

_____

_____

_____

Parent Conference Notes   Date _____

_____

_____

_____

_____

Behavior Documentation Sheet

Student _____ Parent(s) _____

Grade _____ Home Phone _____ Work Phone _____

Date of Entry	+ / ✓	Reason for Documentation Describe the positive or problem behavior. What did you observe? List facts.	Actions Taken with Student Describe in detail disciplinary actions taken or positive reinforcement given.	Parent Contact Note (N) Phone (P) Other (O)	Follow Up Record input received from parent. Describe actions you and parent will take to ensure future success.

Parent Conference Notes   Date _____

_____

_____

_____

_____

_____

Parent Conference Notes   Date _____

_____

_____

_____

_____

_____

Behavior Documentation Sheet

Student_____ Parent(s) _____

Grade _____ Home Phone _____ Work Phone _____

Date of Entry	+ ✓	Reason for Documentation Describe the positive or problem behavior. What did you observe? List facts.	Actions Taken with Student Describe in detail disciplinary actions taken or positive reinforcement given.	Parent Contact Note (N) Phone (P) Other (O)	Follow Up Record input received from parent. Describe actions you and parent will take to ensure future success.

Parent Conference Notes   Date_____

_____

_____

_____

_____

Parent Conference Notes   Date _____

_____

_____

_____

_____

Behavior Documentation Sheet

Student _____ Parent(s) _____

Grade _____ Home Phone _____ Work Phone _____

Date of Entry	+ ✓	**Reason for Documentation** Describe the positive or problem behavior. What did you observe? List facts.	**Actions Taken with Student** Describe in detail disciplinary actions taken or positive reinforcement given.	**Parent Contact** Note (N) Phone (P) Other (O)	**Follow Up** Record input received from parent. Describe actions you and parent will take to ensure future success.

Parent Conference Notes   Date _____

_____

_____

_____

_____

_____

Parent Conference Notes   Date _____

_____

_____

_____

_____

_____

Behavior Documentation Sheet

Student_____ Parent(s)_____

Grade_____Home Phone_____Work Phone_____

Date of Entry	+ ✓	Reason for Documentation Describe the positive or problem behavior. What did you observe? List facts.	Actions Taken with Student Describe in detail disciplinary actions taken or positive reinforcement given.	Parent Contact Note (N) Phone (P) Other (O)	Follow Up Record input received from parent. Describe actions you and parent will take to ensure future success.

Parent Conference Notes   Date_____

_____

_____

_____

_____

Parent Conference Notes   Date_____

_____

_____

_____

_____

Behavior Documentation Sheet

Student_____ Parent(s) _____

Grade _____ Home Phone_____ Work Phone_____

Date of Entry	+ ✓	Reason for Documentation Describe the positive or problem behavior. What did you observe? List facts.	Actions Taken with Student Describe in detail disciplinary actions taken or positive reinforcement given.	Parent Contact Note (N) Phone (P) Other (O)	Follow Up Record input received from parent. Describe actions you and parent will take to ensure future success.

Parent Conference Notes   Date _____

_____

_____

_____

_____

Parent Conference Notes   Date _____

_____

_____

_____

_____

Behavior Documentation Sheet

Student _____ Parent(s) _____

Grade _____ Home Phone _____ Work Phone _____

Date of Entry	+ ✓	Reason for Documentation Describe the positive or problem behavior. What did you observe? List facts.	Actions Taken with Student Describe in detail disciplinary actions taken or positive reinforcement given.	Parent Contact Note (N) Phone (P) Other (O)	Follow Up Record input received from parent. Describe actions you and parent will take to ensure future success.

Parent Conference Notes   Date _____

_____

_____

_____

_____

Parent Conference Notes   Date _____

_____

_____

_____

_____

Behavior Documentation Sheet

Student_____ Parent(s) _____

Grade_____ Home Phone_____ Work Phone_____

Date of Entry	+ ✓	Reason for Documentation Describe the positive or problem behavior. What did you observe? List facts.	Actions Taken with Student Describe in detail disciplinary actions taken or positive reinforcement given.	Parent Contact Note (N) Phone (P) Other (O)	Follow Up Record input received from parent. Describe actions you and parent will take to ensure future success.

Parent Conference Notes   Date _____

_____

_____

_____

_____

Parent Conference Notes   Date _____

_____

_____

_____

_____

Behavior Documentation Sheet

Student_____ Parent(s) _____

Grade_____ Home Phone_____ Work Phone_____

Date of Entry	+ ✓	Reason for Documentation Describe the positive or problem behavior. What did you observe? List facts.	Actions Taken with Student Describe in detail disciplinary actions taken or positive reinforcement given.	Parent Contact Note (N) Phone (P) Other (O)	Follow Up Record input received from parent. Describe actions you and parent will take to ensure future success.

Parent Conference Notes   Date_____

_____

_____

_____

_____

_____

Parent Conference Notes   Date_____

_____

_____

_____

_____

_____

Behavior Documentation Sheet

Student_____ Parent(s) _____

Grade _____ Home Phone _____ Work Phone _____

Date of Entry	+ / ✓	Reason for Documentation: Describe the positive or problem behavior. What did you observe? List facts.	Actions Taken with Student: Describe in detail disciplinary actions taken or positive reinforcement given.	Parent Contact: Note (N) Phone (P) Other (O)	Follow Up: Record input received from parent. Describe actions you and parent will take to ensure future success.

Parent Conference Notes   Date _____

_____
_____
_____
_____
_____

Parent Conference Notes   Date _____

_____
_____
_____
_____
_____

Behavior Documentation Sheet

Student_____ Parent(s)_____

Grade_____ Home Phone_____ Work Phone_____

Date of Entry	+ ✓	**Reason for Documentation** Describe the positive or problem behavior. What did you observe? List facts.	**Actions Taken with Student** Describe in detail disciplinary actions taken or positive reinforcement given.	**Parent Contact** Note (N) Phone (P) Other (O)	**Follow Up** Record input received from parent. Describe actions you and parent will take to ensure future success.

Parent Conference Notes   Date_____

_____

_____

_____

_____

Parent Conference Notes   Date_____

_____

_____

_____

_____

Behavior Documentation Sheet

Student_____ Parent(s)_____

Grade_____ Home Phone_____ Work Phone_____

Date of Entry	+ ✓	**Reason for Documentation** Describe the positive or problem behavior. What did you observe? List facts.	**Actions Taken with Student** Describe in detail disciplinary actions taken or positive reinforcement given.	**Parent Contact** Note (N) Phone (P) Other (O)	**Follow Up** Record input received from parent. Describe actions you and parent will take to ensure future success.

Parent Conference Notes   Date _____   **Parent Conference Notes**   Date _____

_____   _____

_____   _____

_____   _____

_____   _____

_____   _____

Behavior Documentation Sheet

Student_____ Parent(s) _____

Grade_____ Home Phone_____ Work Phone_____

Date of Entry	+ ✓	Reason for Documentation Describe the positive or problem behavior. What did you observe? List facts.	Actions Taken with Student Describe in detail disciplinary actions taken or positive reinforcement given.	Parent Contact Note (N) Phone (P) Other (O)	Follow Up Record input received from parent. Describe actions you and parent will take to ensure future success.

Parent Conference Notes   Date_____

_____

_____

_____

_____

Parent Conference Notes   Date_____

_____

_____

_____

_____

Behavior Documentation Sheet

Student_____ Parent(s)_____

Grade_____ Home Phone_____ Work Phone_____

Date of Entry	+ ✓	Reason for Documentation Describe the positive or problem behavior. What did you observe? List facts.	Actions Taken with Student Describe in detail disciplinary actions taken or positive reinforcement given.	Parent Contact Note (N) Phone (P) Other (O)	Follow Up Record input received from parent. Describe actions you and parent will take to ensure future success.

Parent Conference Notes   **Date**_____

_____

_____

_____

_____

Parent Conference Notes   **Date**_____

_____

_____

_____

_____

Behavior Documentation Sheet

Student_____ Parent(s) _____

Grade_____ Home Phone_____ Work Phone_____

Date of Entry	+ ✓	**Reason for Documentation** Describe the positive or problem behavior. What did you observe? List facts.	**Actions Taken with Student** Describe in detail disciplinary actions taken or positive reinforcement given.	**Parent Contact** Note (N) Phone (P) Other (O)	**Follow Up** Record input received from parent. Describe actions you and parent will take to ensure future success.

Parent Conference Notes   Date_____

_____
_____
_____
_____

Parent Conference Notes   Date_____

_____
_____
_____
_____

Behavior Documentation Sheet

Student_____ Parent(s)_____

Grade_____ Home Phone_____ Work Phone_____

Date of Entry	+ ✓	Reason for Documentation Describe the positive or problem behavior. What did you observe? List facts.	Actions Taken with Student Describe in detail disciplinary actions taken or positive reinforcement given.	Parent Contact Note (N) Phone (P) Other (O)	Follow Up Record input received from parent. Describe actions you and parent will take to ensure future success.

Parent Conference Notes   **Date**_____

_____

_____

_____

_____

Parent Conference Notes   **Date**_____

_____

_____

_____

_____

Behavior Documentation Sheet

Student _____ Parent(s) _____

Grade _____ Home Phone _____ Work Phone _____

Date of Entry	+ ✓	**Reason for Documentation** Describe the positive or problem behavior. What did you observe? List facts.	**Actions Taken with Student** Describe in detail disciplinary actions taken or positive reinforcement given.	**Parent Contact** Note (N) Phone (P) Other (O)	**Follow Up** Record input received from parent. Describe actions you and parent will take to ensure future success.

Parent Conference Notes   Date _____

_____

_____

_____

_____

Parent Conference Notes   Date _____

_____

_____

_____

_____

Behavior Documentation Sheet

Student _____ Parent(s) _____

Grade _____ Home Phone _____ Work Phone _____

Date of Entry	+ ✓	Reason for Documentation Describe the positive or problem behavior. What did you observe? List facts.	Actions Taken with Student Describe in detail disciplinary actions taken or positive reinforcement given.	Parent Contact Note (N) Phone (P) Other (O)	Follow Up Record input received from parent. Describe actions you and parent will take to ensure future success.

Parent Conference Notes   Date _____

_____

_____

_____

_____

_____

Parent Conference Notes   Date _____

_____

_____

_____

_____

_____

Behavior Documentation Sheet

Student_____   Parent(s) _____

Grade_____ Home Phone_____   Work Phone_____

Date of Entry	+ / ✓	**Reason for Documentation** Describe the positive or problem behavior. What did you observe? List facts.	**Actions Taken with Student** Describe in detail disciplinary actions taken or positive reinforcement given.	**Parent Contact** Note (N) Phone (P) Other (O)	**Follow Up** Record input received from parent. Describe actions you and parent will take to ensure future success.

Parent Conference Notes   Date_____

_____

_____

_____

_____

Parent Conference Notes   Date_____

_____

_____

_____

_____

Behavior Documentation Sheet

Student _____ Parent(s) _____

Grade _____ Home Phone _____ Work Phone _____

Date of Entry	+ ✓	Reason for Documentation Describe the positive or problem behavior. What did you observe? List facts.	Actions Taken with Student Describe in detail disciplinary actions taken or positive reinforcement given.	Parent Contact Note (N) Phone (P) Other (O)	Follow Up Record input received from parent. Describe actions you and parent will take to ensure future success.

Parent Conference Notes   Date _____

_____

_____

_____

_____

Parent Conference Notes   Date _____

_____

_____

_____

_____

Behavior Documentation Sheet

Student_____ Parent(s) _____

Grade_____ Home Phone_____ Work Phone_____

Date of Entry	+ ✓	Reason for Documentation Describe the positive or problem behavior. What did you observe? List facts.	Actions Taken with Student Describe in detail disciplinary actions taken or positive reinforcement given.	Parent Contact Note (N) Phone (P) Other (O)	Follow Up Record input received from parent. Describe actions you and parent will take to ensure future success.

Parent Conference Notes   **Date**_____   **Parent Conference Notes**   **Date** _____

_____   _____

_____   _____

_____   _____

_____   _____

_____   _____

Behavior Documentation Sheet

Student_____   Parent(s) _____

Grade _____ Home Phone _____   Work Phone _____

Date of Entry	+ ✓	Reason for Documentation Describe the positive or problem behavior. What did you observe? List facts.	Actions Taken with Student Describe in detail disciplinary actions taken or positive reinforcement given.	Parent Contact Note (N) Phone (P) Other (O)	Follow Up Record input received from parent. Describe actions you and parent will take to ensure future success.

Parent Conference Notes   Date _____

_____

_____

_____

_____

Parent Conference Notes   Date _____

_____

_____

_____

_____

Behavior Documentation Sheet

Student_____ Parent(s)_____

Grade_____ Home Phone_____ Work Phone_____

Date of Entry	+ ✓	Reason for Documentation Describe the positive or problem behavior. What did you observe? List facts.	Actions Taken with Student Describe in detail disciplinary actions taken or positive reinforcement given.	Parent Contact Note (N) Phone (P) Other (O)	Follow Up Record input received from parent. Describe actions you and parent will take to ensure future success.

Parent Conference Notes   Date_____

_____

_____

_____

_____

Parent Conference Notes   Date_____

_____

_____

_____

_____

PARENT COMMUNICATION RESOURCES

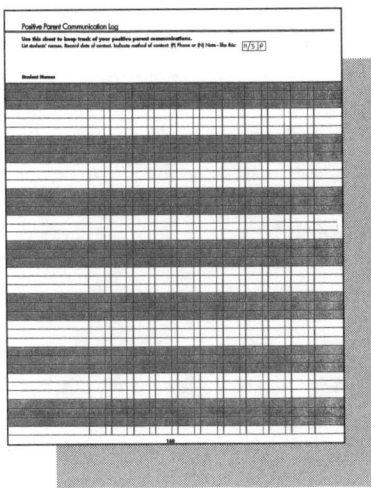

How to develop effective partnerships with parents

- Positive phone calls and notes
- Successful parent conferences
- Contacting parents when problems arise
- Working with parents to solve persistent problems

SECTION THREE

Communicating with Parents All Year Long!

Make a commitment before the school year begins to establish and maintain productive parent communication all year long.

Positive Communication: The Earlier, the Better!

- If possible, phone each parent before school begins to introduce yourself. The message you send is clear—"I care about your child."

- Before school begins, or during the first week of school, send home a letter expressing your hopes and plans for the upcoming school year.

- During the first few weeks of school, send home a positive note or make a phone call to each parent, detailing a success their child has had in school. "Nicki completed all her classwork the first week of school. You should be proud of such responsible behavior."

Planning Makes It Happen

- Use the Parent Communication Logs on pages 159 and 160 to keep track of your positive communication. Plan to make a specific number of positive phone calls each day. (Just two calls a day reach 40 parents in a month.)

- Reproduce an ample supply of positive notes and keep them handy. Take a few minutes when students return from lunch recess to jot down some positive notes. (Three notes a day reach 60 parents a month.) **Note:** Write positive communication time into your daily lesson plans. When positives are scheduled, they happen!

A Few Pointers about Positive Communication

- Be specific when describing a student's positive behavior, talent or accomplishment. "Robert contributed many interesting facts about whales during our science discussion today."

- Put your feelings into the message. Describe how you feel about the student's positive behavior. "It's such a pleasure to have Robert in class. His joyous enthusiasm stimulates interest and creativity in other students."

- Share the joy. Ask the parent to share the content of your conversation (or note) with the student. "Please tell Robert that I called and that I am very pleased with his participation in class."

- Thank parents for their support. Parents help in so many ways—encouraging, nudging, and supporting their child's efforts. Make sure you acknowledge their help with an appreciative word.

Conducting Effective Parent Conferences

Regularly scheduled parent conferences are the perfect time to build solid working relationships with parents. The information you have gathered during the term and recorded on the academic and behavior sheets in your *Record Book Plus* will be the core of your conference. You have at your fingertips the grades, comments and written observations that comprise an accurate account of the experiences that have shaped each student's life at school for the past reporting period.

How to Prepare for a Parent Conference

- Send home conference invitations that explain the purpose of the conference, offer parents flexible time choices and ask parents to suggest specific topics or concerns they wish to discuss.

- Keep a schedule of conferences on which to record all appointment responses.

- Plan for parents' needs by having adult-sized chairs available—both at the conference table and outside the classroom door. Post a schedule on the door indicating your name, room number and the scheduled appointments for the day.

- Gather samples of each student's classwork. Make a folder for each student containing representative work samples (writing journals, daily assignments, projects, reports, tests) to show parents when discussing their child's skills, strengths and weaknesses.

- Gather all academic and behavior documentation. Along with the report card, have your *Record Book Plus* handy.

- Plan what you will say to parents. (Refer to page 150 for step-by-step conference guidance.)

How to Conduct a Successful Parent Conference.

- Greet the parent warmly at the door and usher him or her to a seat.

- Look the parent in the eyes when speaking and address the parent often by name. Make a positive remark about the student early in the conference.

- Refer to the student's work folder and your *Record Book Plus* documentation sheets when making specific points about academics or behavior.

- Explain report card categories and ambiguous or unfamiliar phrases (such as "social skills" and "initiates independent projects").

- Distribute academic and study tips to parents.

- Ask for parent support when addressing specific academic and behavior problems. Stress the importance of teamwork.

- Inform the parent of upcoming reports, projects, field trips or activities.

- End the conference on time and schedule another one if needed. Thank the parent(s) for their support and encourage continuing communication between home and school.

- Record conference notes on the student's Behavior Documentation Sheet.

What to Say During a Parent Conference

Carefully chosen words, a positive and sensitive tone, a professional manner—these can make the difference between a successful parent conference and an unsuccessful one. Follow these sequential guidelines and you'll be on the road to your most successful parent conferences ever.

1 **Begin the conference by giving an example of the student's unique qualities.** "Kerri is an avid reader. When she completes her classwork, she always seems to have a library book in her hand."

2 **Update the parent on any previous problems.** "Kerri is doing much better with her division facts. On her last timed math test she scored 95%."

3 **Discuss the student's academic strengths.** "You can see from her writing samples that Kerri continues to be an imaginative writer. Her stories are filled with vivid descriptions and her vocabulary is expanding daily."

4 **Get parent input on the student's academic performance.** "Does Kerri have any problems (medical, emotional, social) that might effect her academic performance?"

5 **Discuss your academic goals for the remainder of the school year.** "By the end of the year, Kerri should be able to multiply two-digit numbers and compute division problems with remainders."

6 **Present the social strengths of the student.** "Kerri is sensitive to the feelings of others. Last week she wrote a comforting note to a classmate whose cat had run away."

7 **If appropriate, discuss the student's weaknesses in social interactions.** Offer a plan of action in which you and the parent will work together. "I'd like to see Kerri interact more with others when working in a group. She has great ideas, but is rather shy about contributing them. I will involve her in partner activities at school to build her confidence. You might want to ask for Kerri's input at home when making decisions that involve her. This should build her self-confidence, too."

8 **Discuss your goals for the student's social development for the remainder of the school year.** "As Kerri begins to gain confidence, I will encourage her to take more leadership roles in group activities."

9 **Get parent input regarding the student's social behavior.** "What can you tell me about Kerri's interactions with children outside of school?"

Contacting Parents at the First Sign of a Problem

The most common complaint from parents is that they are not informed about problems soon enough. When is it time to contact a parent about a behavior or academic problem? The answer is simple—the sooner, the better!

Involving parents from the start will help you solve many problems before they get out of hand.

When Should You Involve Parents?

If you are in doubt as to whether a situation warrants parent involvement, try this simple test:

The "Your Own Child" Test

When a problem arises at school, ask yourself the following questions:

• If this were my child, would I want to know about the problem, and would I want to know immediately?

• If this were my child, would this information help me understand my child and be able to help him/her more effectively?

If you answer yes to any of these questions, it is time to contact the parent.

Tips for Contacting Parents about a Problem

1 Before speaking to a parent, write down what you plan to say.

2 The quickest, easiest way to contact a parent is by telephone. By dialing the number, you are dealing with the problem in the most efficient way possible.

3 Keep your conversation short and to the point. Clearly explain the situation, get parent input and answer any questions the parent may have.

4 To explain the problem in objective, observable terms, always have your student documentation sheets (academic and behavior) with you when speaking to parents.

5 If the problem continues, arrange to meet with the parent(s) for a problem-solving conference. (See page 152.)

Working with Parents to Solve Persistent Problems

If your initial contact with a parent doesn't solve the academic or behavior problem, it is time to arrange a problem-solving conference with the parent.

The purpose of this conference is to work together to find solutions to the student's problem and to provide the parent with all the tools necessary to ensure successful follow-up and follow-through at home. Your thorough and objective comments on the behavior and academic documentation sheets will be an invaluable source of information for the conference.

Preparation Is the Key to a Successful Problem-Solving Conference.

Follow these guidelines when preparing for a problem-solving conference:

1 **Decide who should be involved in the conference.**

The teacher and the parents are the backbone of the conference, but you might consider including these people for any input or assistance they might offer:

- the student
- the principal
- resource personnel
- a counselor
- the nurse
- a translator

2 **Choose appropriate documentation that conveys the problem. Documentation should detail all actions that have taken place regarding this problem. Gather documentation from a variety of sources:**

- Behavior Documentation Sheet
- Grading sheets
- Work samples (for academic problems)
- Other notes, phone logs and parent communications that are pertinent to the problem

3 **Plan what you will say at the conference.**

Your conference will be more productive if you plan your presentation ahead of time. A professional, positive, sensitive manner will help you gain the parent's trust. A sense of teamwork and the confidence that the problem can be worked out will gain you the parent support you need.

Note: See the sample problem-solving conference on pages 153-154 for specific ideas on what to say to parents. Use the parent conference planning sheet (page 155) to help you plan individual conference material.

Sample Problem-Solving Conference

1 **Begin with a statement of concern, updating the situation.**

"Mrs. Brown, I'm very concerned about Eric's misbehavior in class. It has not changed since I spoke to you last week."

2 **Describe the specific problem in detail.** Present the information you have documented on the Behavior Documentation Sheet.

"You can see from these records that in the past week Eric has shouted out in class three times and has thrown his pencil at another student on two occasions."

3 **Describe what you have done.** As you refer to the entries on the Behavior Documentation Sheet, explain previous attempts to deal with the problem.

"As you know from my notes and phone calls, Eric received a warning about his behavior on Monday. He and I discussed appropriate behavior and the ways I will recognize that appropriate behavior. Tuesday, Eric was benched during recess to write a brief essay on the disruptive influence of shouting out in class. You signed that paper Tuesday night. On Wednesday, Eric threw pencils at two classmates. Because of the potential danger in his actions, Eric was sent to the principal and you were contacted for this problem-solving conference."

4 **Get parental input on the problem.**

"Has Eric had similar problems in the past? Does he have similar problems at home? Is there something happening outside of school that may be affecting his behavior?"

5 **Get parental input on how to solve the problem.**

"How do you feel we can work together to help Eric solve this problem?"

6 **Tell the parent what actions you will take to solve the problem.** Explain your new plan of action. Check to make sure that the parent understands clearly.

"Mrs. Brown, since this problem has continued, I am going to change the disciplinary consequences for Eric. From now on, each time he shouts out in class, he will be sent to the principal immediately and you will be called. He won't receive any more warnings and no preliminary consequences will be given. In addition, I will praise Eric often and recognize him when he *is* behaving properly. I will send home a positive note each day that he behaves responsibly."

7 **Explain what you need the parent to do at home to solve the problem.** Carefully explain what you need the parent to do. Listen for any reservations the parent may express. Make sure the parent understands exactly what you are asking. The parent's commitment is essential for the child's success.

"Mrs. Brown, we need to work together to help Eric improve his behavior. His shouting out in class and throwing objects is completely unacceptable. Any time you are called at home about this problem, I'd like you to follow through with your own disciplinary measures. Taking away privileges such as using the phone or watching TV can be very effective. Whatever you choose to do, remember that you must do it consistently. Most importantly, please give Eric lots of praise when he brings home the positive notes. You might even reward an entire week of good behavior with a special privilege or treat."

(Continued on next page)

8 **Let the parent know that you are confident that the problem can be worked out.** Use the word "confident" to reassure the parent of your experience and capability.

"I am confident, Mrs. Brown, that together we can make this a better year for Eric. I've dealt with many children with similar problems, and I can assure you that we will be able to turn things around if we are united in our efforts."

9 **Tell the parent that there will be follow-up contact from you.** A parent needs to know that you are going to stay involved. Provide this reassurance by giving a specific date for a follow-up call or note.

"Mrs. Brown, I will be calling you this Friday evening to let you know how things are working out for Eric."

10 **Recap the conference.** Write down all plans agreed upon. Record these action plans on the student's Behavior Documentation Sheet. Give a copy of the plans to the parent.

11 **Close the conference.** Thank the parent for meeting with you, and encourage him or her to contact you with any problems. Stress once again the importance of working together as a team for the student's success.

Problem-Solving Conference Planning Sheet

Teacher _____   Grade _____   Date of Conference _____

Student _____   Parent or Guardian _____

1. Begin with a statement of concern, updating the situation. _____
   _____

2. Describe the specific problem and present the Behavior Documentation Sheet. _____
   _____

3. Describe what you have already done to solve the problem. _____
   _____

4. Get parental input on the problem. _____
   Remarks: _____
   _____

5. Get parental input on how to solve the problem.
   Remarks: _____
   _____

6. Tell the parent what actions you plan to take to solve the problem. _____
   _____

7. Explain what you need the parent to do at home to support these problem-solving actions. ____
   _____

8. Let the parent know that you are confident that the problem can be worked out. _____
   _____

9. Tell the parent that there will be follow-up contact from you. _____
   _____

10. Review the conference. _____
    _____

Notes: _____
_____
_____
_____
_____

How to Handle Difficult Situations with Parents

Sooner or later you will encounter parents who are uncooperative.

Parents become angry, frustrated or overwhelmed for many reasons. They may direct hostility and criticism toward you during a problem-solving conference or catch you off guard with unexpected phone calls or unscheduled school visits.

Be prepared for these unsettling situations.

Remember to remain calm and always present yourself as a professional working in the best interest of your students.

Turn Difficult Situations into Productive Problem-Solving Encounters.

Whenever a difficult situation arises (at conference time, on the phone, or during a parent's unscheduled visit to school), follow these communication strategies to develop a more positive relationship with parents.

1 **Listen attentively to the parent's complaints.**

Parent: "Marissa came home today in tears. She said you picked on her during class and then gave her extra math to do tonight because she didn't finish her work during class."

2 **Show your empathy and concern by asking for more specific information about the complaint.** This shows that you are able to handle criticism and maintain control of the conversation.

Teacher: "I'm sorry to hear that Marissa came home in tears. Can you be more specific about how Marissa says that I picked on her during class? Did she say why she must finish her math assignment at home tonight?"

Note: If the parent's concern or criticism is justified, accept your mistake. Don't make excuses or place blame on others. Answer the parent honestly and make your statement clearly.

For example:

Parent: "When Manuel came home from school today, he told me that you had lowered his science grade for not turning in his homework assignment. I know he did that assignment. I checked it last night and saw him put the paper in his backpack. I'm very upset!"

Teacher: "You have reason to be upset, Mr. Rodriguez. After Manuel left school today, I found his science paper in the back of my record book. It was my fault. I had misplaced the paper. I'm very sorry about the mix-up."

---

3 **If the criticism or complaint is partially or totally incorrect, direct the conversation toward parent realization and acceptance of the truth**. Keep focused on your goals. If the parent steers away from the real issues with criticism or threats, refocus the conversation by:

- restating the problem behavior,

- telling the parent you understand his or her concerns, and

- repeating your goal for the conversation.

Parent: "I wish you and everyone else at school would stop giving Marissa such a hard time. Every day she comes home telling me how you or the kids in her class are picking on her and getting her all upset. This never happened at Marissa's old school!"

Teacher: "I understand that you feel Marissa is being unjustly treated, but we need to focus on the facts. My documentation on Marissa shows the behavior choices she made today. When I asked for papers to be turned in at the end of math period, Marissa said that she had lost her paper. A search turned up her incomplete paper, covered with doodling, in the trash can. Marissa spent afternoon recess on the bench working on her assignment. Because she didn't finish it at recess, she was assigned the paper as homework. We need to find out why Marissa chose not to do her work during class."

If the parent continues to argue or focus on different goals, try this simple but effective refocusing technique. Just keep repeating your goal without being sidetracked by the parent's comments.

Parent: "Marissa says that you are *always* picking on her in front of others. I want something done about this!"

Teacher: "I understand your concern, Mrs. Jones, but we must focus on how to help Marissa become more responsible about completing her classwork and following the rules."

Parent: "Like I've told you, we never had this problem at her other school."

Teacher: "I understand what you are saying, Mrs. Jones, but that's not the point. Marissa is choosing not to do her work and we must discover why, and how we can help her."

Note: This refocusing technique should be used only when a parent is trying to divert you in a manipulative way. If the parent brings up a legitimate concern that is vital to the solution of the problem, don't use this technique. It will only serve to cut off important communication.

If a parent attempts to shift the responsibility for the child's poor behavior to you, use the "wrong person" technique. This technique is very effective in helping a parent focus on the real issues.

Parent: "Marissa doesn't have time to do her math tonight. She has soccer practice from five until eight."

Teacher: "I understand that you are upset, Mrs. Jones, but you are upset with the wrong person. The person you should be upset with is Marissa because she chose not to do her work in class today."

(Continued on next page)

6 **If a parent is misinformed, point out the facts.** After listening to the parent's comments, point out in a gentle but firm way what actually happened in factual, observable terms.

Teacher: "Mrs. Jones, I understand that Marissa says she was singled out and embarrassed in front of the entire class. I understand that she may feel that way, but here is what happened. When I discovered that Marissa had thrown her paper away, I took her aside and quietly told her that she would have to miss afternoon recess to work on her math paper. When I saw that the paper was still unfinished after recess, I asked her in private to stay after school a few minutes. I assigned the math paper as homework and told Marissa that I would be calling you this afternoon."

7 **If the parent is still angry, point out that conflict between the two of you is harmful to the student and won't solve the problem.**

Teacher: "I know we don't see eye-to-eye on this issue, but we're not going to help Marissa if we don't work together. We both want the best for Marissa."

8 **Finally, if the parent is still upset, suggest that he or she talk with the principal.** Do not allow a critical parent to continue criticizing you. If it is clear that the parent is not going to calm down, it is appropriate to have the parent talk to the principal. (Just bringing up this alternative may calm the parent down.)

Teacher: "It seems as though you and I cannot resolve this issue, so maybe you should speak with the principal about it."

Note: What to Do When an Upset Parent Phones or Visits You Unexpectedly

After giving the parent a chance to express his or her concerns, let the parent know that these matters are too important to discuss in haste. Set a time with the parent to talk about the problem in detail, either in a face-to-face conference or over the phone. Thank the parent for being concerned.

Teacher: "Mrs. Ryan, I want to thank you for coming to me with your concerns. Making sure that Patty's assignments are appropriate is very important to me. I'd like to set up a meeting to discuss the matter when we have more time. Would tomorrow afternoon be good for you?"

sitive Parent Communication Log

this sheet to keep track of your positive parent communications.

students' names. Record date of contact. Indicate method of contact: (P) Phone or (N) Note - like this:

11/3	P

dent Names

Positive Parent Communication Log

Use this sheet to keep track of your positive parent communications.

List students' names. Record date of contact. Indicate method of contact: (P) Phone or (N) Note - like this: | 11/3 | P |

Student Names